How to Become an
EMERGENCY
RESPONSE
DRIVER

Fire | Ambulance | Police

Bill Lavender

THE ULTIMATE GUIDE TO BECOMING AN EMERGENCY RESPONSE DRIVER

Orders: Please contact How2Become Ltd, Suite 1, 60 Churchill Square Business Centre, Kings Hill, Kent ME19 4YU.

You can order through Amazon.co.uk under ISBN 978-1-910602-55-3, via the website www.How2Become.com or through Gardners.com.

ISBN: 978-1-910602-55-3

First published in 2015 by How2Become Ltd.

Fifth Edition – 2019

Typeset for How2Become Ltd by Anton Pshinka.

CREDITS

A special thank you to:

- The Police Foundation and The Stationery Office (TSO) for their very kind permission to quote references from "Roadcraft" - The Police Drivers' Handbook

- The many emergency response instructors, working nationwide within the ambulance service, for all their thoughts, suggestions and advice.

- Serving and retired colleagues from the police and fire services for their valuable input

- Steve Wright at **Hangar 18 Custom Art** for his graphic vehicle drawings

Further reading:

- Roadcraft – The Police Drivers' Handbook (TSO)
- The Highway Code – (TSO)
- The Official DVSA Guide to Better Driving – Driver Vehicle Standards Agency (TSO)
- UK Ambulance Services Emergency Response Drivers' Handbook - Association of Ambulance Chief Executives (AACE)
- Human Aspects of Police Driving - Dr Gordon Sharp, along with publications on driver behaviour by Dr Lisa Dorn
- The Chimp Paradox - Prof Steve Peters
- Hughes - eGuide to Traffic Law
- Relevant Service Organisational Policies and Protocols

Disclaimer:

Any views or opinions expressed in this publication are entirely those of the author. They are not intended to represent those of any emergency service, including the London Ambulance Service (LAS).

The onus of having the satisfactory knowledge, driving skill and understanding to make appropriate interpretations, rests with the response driver in the circumstances encountered while driving. No liability whatsoever can be accepted by the author for any misinterpretation of the contents of this book.

mydriving.co.uk

Scan the Quick Response (QR) Code below to visit the "My Driving" website established in 1996 by Bill Lavender. To do this, download and use the app on your mobile phone or tablet. Easy!

This was one of the first UK driving websites, designed as an information resource intended for all drivers. Register on this independent site and you will find:

- Any necessary technical updates to this booklet

- Colour versions of all the diagrams and illustrations included here

Also visit driving4tomorrow.com

This website is owned by Chris Gilbert, former Class One advanced driver and instructor at the Metropolitan Police Motor Driving School (MPMDS) at Hendon. It promotes educational DVDs that will help every driver, including aspiring emergency response drivers to learn and develop the skill of commentary driving. You can also book (non-response) driving days with Chris. Just scan the QR code from your mobile phone or tablet and you're there!

Welcome to the Fifth Edition of

"How to become an Emergency Response Driver"

Bill Lavender – almost 40 years of combined industry experience across all vehicle categories, including front line emergency services.

Also author of
"How to become a Driving Instructor"

Everything you need to know to qualify as a DVSA Approved Driving Instructor

CONTENTS

FOREWORD by Chris Gilbert, former Class 1 Advanced Driver and Driving Instructor at the Metropolitan Police Motor Driving School (MPMDS) Hendon, London.

It is a privilege to be invited to commend Bill Lavender's book 'How to become an Emergency Response Driver'. This guide will be very helpful to students about to embark on a Standard Response Course, which involves blue light driving. This type of training is usually provided by the emergency services – Police, Ambulance, Fire, and Military. These services often employ and train civilian driving instructors for this role.

I have known Bill for twenty five years and I know him to be a man of integrity and high standards, who is dedicated to the enhancement of teaching skills within the driver training world. To that end, Bill continues to write training articles for industry magazines such as "Intelligent Instructor". His monthly feature, teaching targets is aimed at ADIs as well as new driving instructors who wish to develop their instructional and coaching skills. Bill's first publication, "How to become a driving instructor" is another example of his simple and easy style. Both theoretically and practically, this has guided many aspiring new instructors, especially with the final practical DVSA test, the "Part 3" which still remains the hardest to pass.

Bill became an ADI in 1982 and spent most of his early career at the British School of Motoring (BSM) in various senior training and development roles including Learning Resource Controller. Bill Lavender is currently employed as a driving tutor by the London Ambulance Service (LAS) where he continues to be an influence on the driving standards of 999 blue light ambulance drivers.

With his academic and teaching background, combined with almost ten years of blue light instructional experience, Bill is ideally placed to write "How to become an Emergency Response Driver".

A driver of an Emergency Response Vehicle needs to consider every other road user and drive to the best of their ability, so that the vehicle is always in the best position, travelling at the right speed, with the right gear engaged. On top of all this, they need to make sure that they arrive on the scene as rapidly as possible. The successful Emergency Response Driver considers everything and leaves nothing to chance. The basis of all Emergency Response Driving is a very high standard of Roadcraft.

I often receive enquiries from ADIs seeking information about how to become an Emergency Response Driving Instructor (ERDI). First I say this, being a 'L' driving instructor is poles apart from being an Emergency Response Driving Instructor (ERDI). A much higher standard of driving with advanced driving skills is necessary to instruct and to demonstrate 999 driving. I would suggest the minimum standard to start training as an ERDI is an Institute of Advanced Motorists Masters test pass at Distinction Level (80% or higher). Within the police service, it has been my experience when road testing applicants for the post of Civilian Driving Instructor that it is likely their standard of driving will fall below the standard required.

Therefore, my recommendation to anyone wishing to become an Emergency Response Driver or Instructor, is learn Roadcraft, improve your driving skills with commentary, and read Bill's book 'How to become an Emergency Response Driver', which I commend highly.

Chris Gilbert
2019

INTRODUCTION

To become an emergency response driver, you first need a career path into one of the emergency services. The main organisations that require emergency response drivers are of course the police, ambulance and fire services. Other organisations whose employees might have a response role include the National Blood Service and search and rescue organisations, including the Coastguard service and Lifeboat, Mountain and Cave Rescue. Military vehicle drivers, for instance those involved in wartime bomb disposal, will also be expected to participate in emergency response.

Emergency response driving with the exemptions to road traffic law is a great privilege, extremely rewarding but ultimately a huge responsibility. Once fully qualified, driving with the use of blues and twos must continue to be considered as a privilege and not an entitlement. There are no exemptions for careless or dangerous driving.

The ability to drive on blues and twos is only afforded to employees who need this role as a condition of employment. At the moment there are no formal requirements for people driving emergency response vehicles to be trained beyond an ordinary driving licence. The emergency services do, however, recognise the need to deliver training in-house or through outsourcing. Depending on the particular service, the level of theory, delivered in the classroom may vary - as may the on/off road practical elements.

In all cases, it is necessary that potential emergency response drivers first receive training and development in non-response advanced driving. Chapters Six and Seven the essential technical details for this. It is not enough to just to read this information; intending response drivers will need coaching by a suitably qualified specialist driving instructor, who will measure and then develop your previous driving experience.

Whether driving on response or non-response, you must minimise the risk taken when dealing with hazards. Having a positive attitude means taking on responsibility and ownership of the driving tasks. In effect, this means not blaming anybody or anything else for your own errors or misjudgements.

This guide has been written with all emergency response drivers in mind. However there is some focus on the training and development requirements of the ambulance service, where theoretical knowledge makes an important contribution to their qualifying examination.

Within each emergency service there are some differences, although they use the same legal exemptions. The police, for instance, have three levels of police driver – basic, standard response and advanced. The ambulance and fire services have only one level. In Appendix Four and Five there is some detail regarding police and fire service training.

In all services, your programme of training is likely to begin with a non-response assessment drive usually referred to as the ITN (Identify Training Needs) drive. Your performance will most probably be graded and a pre-scheduled course will be adapted to suit your learning needs.

Formative and summative assessment

To ensure the effectiveness of training, theory and practical checks will be conducted. These will normally be formative assessments, designed to identify and meet any development needs.

The aim is to achieve an attitude that nothing less than the highest standard of driving behaviour is acceptable. The manner in which emergency vehicles are driven, whether routinely or on response, has a direct bearing on public perception of the emergency services. The importance of this should be self-evident for a professional driver. Where a student is unable or unwilling to drive systematically and correctly on non-response routine driving, the necessary skills are unlikely to improve when on an emergency call using blues and twos. Continuous formative assessment, with feedback during training, using "action plans" will normally resolve any ongoing development issues. Success does depend on the student taking full ownership and responsibility for their own learning and performance.

Throughout the emergency services there is a strong ethos that all drivers have an excellent command of the Highway Code. In the ambulance industry, an important part of this requirement is a thorough knowledge of road traffic signs. New ambulance drivers are expected to learn and know the exact definitions of all the traffic signs published in the "Highway Code" and "Know Your Traffic Signs".

Since January 2016, the Awarding Body, "FutureQuals" has taken over responsibility for the accreditation of ambulance driver qualifications. Assessments of both theoretical and practical driving are now based on learning outcomes agreed with the national "Driver Training Advisory Group" known as DTAG. (DTAG represents the statutory ambulance services). These outcomes are incorporated in Appendix Three of this publication.

NHS Trusts and most private services use this criteria for formative assessment. As well as completing an evidence portfolio, to complete the award, all students must undergo an independent practical check of blue-light driving competency. The Performance Criteria for this is based on the High Speed Driver Training (HSDT) competencies (Appendix One).

A summative assessment is carried out by a different driving instructor using a criteria based the five elements of High Speed Driver Training explained in Appendix One. Any serious errors or frequently repeated mistakes committed during the assessment will result in a "deferral". Any outstanding deferrals from the programme must be resolved in order to demonstrate competence.

Emergency response driving criteria

The practical standard set in Appendix One is not a training course in itself. The intention is that it provides the essential minimum learning outcomes that any training course for Emergency Response Drivers must achieve. The standard provides the basis for the practical and theoretical assessment of Emergency Response Drivers, with the intention of ensuring a degree of uniformity across all the emergency services. The nine points below list the practical essentials of emergency driving:

1. Demonstrate the correct operation and application of all emergency visual and warning devices – "Always uses devices appropriately with suitable variation"

2. Observe all non-exemptions whilst driving on an emergency – "Excellent knowledge and adherences at all times"

3. Demonstrate the application and justification of emergency exemptions whilst driving on an emergency - "Excellent knowledge and adherences at all times"

4. Demonstrate the correct principles and compliance with Road Traffic Law - "Excellent knowledge and adherences at all times"

5. Demonstrate the appropriate attitude to emergency driving – "Always calm and objective, no evidence of aggression, personalisation or red mist"

6. Maintain concentration throughout the emergency drive – "Full and consistent concentration giving a smooth safe drive"

7. Demonstrate accurate safe judgement and consideration at all hazards – "Excellent observation and planning skills demonstrated"

8. Use safe progression when able but reduces speed in accordance with prevailing road and traffic conditions – "Always correct speed for the conditions"

9. Maintain driving standard to the "System of Car Control" as per Roadcraft - "Excellent knowledge and adherences at all times"

Chapter 1

DRIVER RESPONSIBILITY

Staying legal

The most immediate responsibility is to confirm license entitlements to drive the emergency response vehicle. The driver must hold a full DVLA license for the class of vehicle to be driven. Any endorsements or convictions under road traffic legislation must be reported to the appropriate persons as required.

If your eyesight fails to meet the relevant legal requirements, or if there are any medical or adverse conditions that could impair your driving ability; you have a responsibility to report this to the licensing authority.

Being fit to drive on emergency response

Do we feel well enough to drive? Any illness, or medications to treat them could impair driving performance. Feeling angry, tired, depressed or stressed is going to be a major handicap. Do we have a coping strategy if we have any of these feelings? Feeling hungry or thirsty can be a distraction. Plan for this by taking sandwiches and a drink to work.

The right attitude

When driving, we might consider that driving standards are deteriorating and that it's other drivers that are inattentive, discourteous and inconsiderate. It is maybe worth reflecting how our own driving might be seen by others. How alert, courteous and considerate are we - honestly? How tolerant are we of the mistakes, probably quite unintentional, of others?

We might feel that we have great skill controlling the vehicle and good awareness of traffic situations, but is our own behaviour always beyond reproach?

Learning outcomes

Advanced driver training promotes a positive, progressive, smooth and safe driving style. Our expectation is that new response drivers complete the prescribed driving course, not only to formally qualify as advanced drivers, but also become better people. People who understand both the technical complexities of driving a vehicle and also the human factors that influence everyone's attitude when using public roads.

Travelling inside our vehicles, often with all the comforts of home, we feel safe and comfortable. It is here that we might display behaviour we would never dream of showing when outside our vehicles.

There will be demanding times when human psychology, particularly our emotions and peer pressure can be a strong influence on our decision making. This can make positive choices difficult and therefore may compromise safety.

Under supervision during training, our concentration is likely to be high and we will be on our best practical behaviour. We are unlikely to speed intentionally or drive too fast for the conditions. We will comply with all traffic legislation and apply all necessary courtesies and considerations.

Course inputs will improve our theoretical and practical knowledge; we can expect to raise our forward vision and observation. Training will make us become more experienced in the use of the vehicle's controls.

Although it may be obvious that a lack of concentration is a potential cause of collisions; will we ignore this after the completion of our training? If we don't really feel that speeding is dangerous, will we continue to break limits? If it's possible to get away with crossing an amber signal, where it would be safe to stop, why bother stopping?

How much can an advanced driving course influence or even change our attitude towards the subjects taught? Should we be reminded that our driving standard is only as good as our last drive?

We need to recognise the need, and want to drive with the right attitude, for the new learning and understanding to take full effect.

Driving Style

Emergency response driving is undoubtedly a high risk activity.

You are three times more likely to be involved in a collision when responding to an emergency, so, our overriding objective is to arrive safely without creating another emergency incident.

To avoid costly collisions we need to make an honest appraisal of the factors that influence our decisions when driving. It may be that our moods may explain why our driving style changes; but it is our personalities that determine the style that we will stick to most of the time.

We never stop learning. By accepting responsibility to keep looking to improve our knowledge and skills; this will help ensure that we maintain an acceptable driving style for both routine and emergency response driving. If we don't do this, there's a danger that our skill will fade, and our standards will slip, meaning we start paying less attention to safety.

Red Mist

Having received an emergency call, the need to get to our destination in the shortest time may cause "Red Mist". Driving a vehicle on emergency response and claiming the exemptions to road traffic law that we are privileged to enjoy, requires an ability to control this.

We need to keep a relaxed state of mind, concentrating on progressive but safe driving. In practice, this means giving other road users plenty of time to respond to our emergency lights and sirens - we say seven seconds. It also means never getting into any personal conflict with other road users. We might feel very determined to achieve an objective such as catching up quickly and passing any vehicles in front, regardless of other dangers. Our focus has to be on realistically assessing driving risks.

Fixed attention on such a goal can lead to blindness to other potential road and traffic hazards. We have a professional responsibility to check and control any feelings of:

- Impatience – maintain a calm approach to our driving tasks
- Intolerance – of other drivers' apparent inferior observation and anticipation skills
- Aggression – avoid becoming angry when the through way is obstructed
- Impulsiveness – form a risk assessment, consider a Driving Plan B - an alternative route
- Justifying risks – whether it is perhaps testosterone driven pride, or risk taking for a "noble cause", we must not become emotionally or physiologically caught up in the emergency call.

The current edition of the Police Drivers' Handbook "Roadcraft" (Page 16) states it this way:

"Red mist means that your attention is not on your driving but on some specific goal; you have become emotionally and physiologically caught up in the incident.

"Red mist" is a colloquial term used to describe the state of mind of drivers who become determined to achieve some objective on the journey - catching the vehicle in front, or getting to an incident in the shortest possible time. Fixed attention on a particular goal can lead to blindness to other potential hazards, such as pedestrians or other vehicles at intersections. This means a driver is at best less able and at worst no longer capable of realistically assessing driving risks."

Emergency response drivers do not have carte blanche to ignore speed limits or red traffic lights. The exemptions which have been granted are very specific, limited and are enshrined in law. If as a result of exercising those exemptions any collision occurs, the emergency response driver is every bit as liable for the consequences as any other motorist using the road. The courts will have to make their own decision where proceedings are brought in the light of particular circumstances.

Begin to review your own behavioural risk by considering the four levels presented in the "Goals for Driver Education" (GDE) Matrix.

The Goals for Driver Education (GDE) Matrix

The 4 levels that are involved in all driving tasks	Knowledge and skill the driver has to master	Risk-increasing factors the driver must be aware of and be able to avoid	Self-evaluation for continuous development
1. Mastery of vehicle manoeuvring **(Traditional Driver Training)**	The physics of driving. Skill with vehicle handling eg when braking, cornering and accelerating	Risks connected with advanced vehicle technology. Distraction through smart phone use	Personal strengths and weaknesses with basic driving skills when manoeuvring in hazardous situations
2. Mastery of traffic situations **(Traditional Driver Training)**	Applying 'Highway Code'. Observation, Hazard Perception Skills and anticipation	Awareness of poor safety margins, neglect of rules, adverse driving or traffic conditions	Level of hazard perception, from a viewpoint of strengths and weaknesses

The two levels (above) are all that is needed to pass a DVSA driving test. The next two, higher levels reflect the needs of post-test driving training and assessment.

3. Goals and context of driving for a specific journey **(Driver Education & Behaviour)**	Journey related considerations. Effects of goals, environment choice, effects of social pressure, evaluation of necessity	What is the purpose of the journey? What are the conditions likely to be? Who are you carrying? Any social pressures?	How well has the trip been planned? What are the goals, motives, feelings and expectations?
4. Human factors. The goals for life and your skills for living **(Driver Education & Behaviour)**	What are your life goals and values? What's your behavioural style and how does it affect your driving? (Can be based on age, social position / culture)	Risks connected with: social environment & peer pressure to perform a particular way. Lifestyle habits that create driving risk	Awareness of personal tendencies / competence: Impulse control, motives, fatigue, stress, lifestyle and values, coping strategy

Learning outcomes, with training

Emergency Response drivers, during routine driving or when responding to emergencies will:

- Identify the human factors that are significant contributors to road traffic collision

- Accept ownership for maintaining a high standard of professional driving

- Act as a role model of professional driving standards that others should aspire to

- Demonstrate an ability to predict and safely respond to the behavioural changes of other drivers

- Identify situations where conflict involves the response crew and / or other road users

- Be able to manage confrontational behaviour
- Reflect on own driving practice during confrontational behaviour

Emergency Response drivers, when responding to emergencies will:

- Recognise "red mist" – the extreme emotional feelings that can temporarily cloud our judgment

Chapter 2

VEHICLE
DAILY INSPECTION
(VDI)

Emergency vehicles work under arduous conditions. This makes the VDI, which takes place before each shift or when the vehicle is changed, an essential procedure.

- This inspection should take less than ten minutes and is intended to ensure that there are no dangerous or illegal defects.

All drivers have a legal responsibility to ensure that the vehicle is in a roadworthy condition before driving. This responsibility cannot be delegated.

The following checks must be carried out:

1. Vehicle is sitting on ground correctly – no suspension issues
2. Any damage to bodywork or wheels – no sharp edges
3. Tyre condition, including tread depth and pressures. Look out for serious cuts and any other damage
4. Windows and mirrors clear and clean – free from cracks
5. Wiper condition
6. Under the bonnet - Fluid levels: oil, coolant, washer, oil, brake and steering
7. Lights, including brake, indicators and emergency lights
8. Interior lights
9. Horn and sirens working (Check Service Policy on location for testing sirens)
10. On board equipment secure (fire extinguisher and first aid kit, where supplied)
11. Electrical shore-line disconnected

Drivers will be provided with an agreed checklist. Any defects must be reported or remedied before the vehicle is driven. Where a vehicle is unfit for use, ensure that alternative arrangements are made, that are acceptable to all parties.

Different services use many different types of vehicle to suit a variety of purposes. Although not directly a part of the VDI, before driving, ensure that you know whether your vehicle is:

- Front / rear or four wheel drive
- Diesel / petrol or other type of fuel
- Manual or automatic transmission

Again, although not directly part of the VDI, your response vehicle may be fitted with a Mobile Data Terminal (MDT). Using Computer Aided Despatching (CAD) software, the MDT updates jobs and times. It is also likely that your vehicle will have an Automatic Vehicle Locating System (AVLS) for tracking purposes by Service Control.

Increasingly so, response vehicles are also being fitted as standard with Incident Data Recorders (IDR) colloquially known as 'black boxes'. These should be checked for stored incidents at the start of any journey and prior to any movement of the vehicle. An LED will blink on the IDR display if an incident has happened or beeps in the event of a major collision/damage detected. These devices can be interrogated by a laptop computer and will show detailed vehicle data leading up to point of impact including G-force, speed, direction, what emergency equipment was on (if any) and harsh/erratic steering or braking. It is highly likely that all ambulances will be fitted with these devices in the near future. IDR data will be used by collision investigators, particularly where the Road Traffic Collision (RTC) involves a fatality.

Learning outcomes, with training ...

Emergency response drivers need to be able to:

- Demonstrate a Vehicle Daily Inspection (VDI) on a range of vehicles
- Explain briefly the reasons for checking each listed item
- Complete the correct documentation when carrying out the VDI
- State the actions to take if vehicle defects are identified
- Use the MDT or any fitted navigation system
- State the performance capabilities and limitations of a range of vehicles.

Response drivers need to be able to state the statutory requirements when checking a vehicle for:

- Legal compliance
- Safety

Chapter 3

PRE-DRIVING CHECKS (PDC)

Professional driving has to begin with good posture behind the wheel. You need to be comfortable, as well as positioned to reach and operate the controls easily. You need to have an unobstructed view of the road ahead, as well as the sides and rear of the vehicle.

Below is the updated "cockpit drill" that is recommended when driving all ambulance vehicles. There may be some minor variance within each emergency service.

1. Handbrake applied and gear lever in neutral
2. Adjust seat position to ensure reach of steering and controls, also set head restraint
3. Mirrors set for side and rear view
4. Gearbox familiarisation
5. Start vehicle
   - Manual – depress clutch
   - Automatic – depress brake.
   Check all ignition lights
6. Footbrake, static check
7. Handbrake check
8. Gauges, including fuel and switch settings, check navigation
9. Seat belts on and check all doors are closed
10. Brake, mobile check – brake early for first hazard at low speed

You must be completely satisfied that before driving, that your vehicle is roadworthy, so make it a habit:

- When starting the vehicle (Point 5 above), to apply some movement to the steering as well as depressing the clutch/brake. This will check for power steering assistance
- When making a static footbrake check, check that the brake pedal travel is not excessive or feels spongy. The pedal must not fall to the floor.

When performing Point 8 it is particularly important to know the location of all the ancillary (minor) controls such as for warm air and demister settings; air conditioning; headlights; horn; windscreen washers and wipers.

Although not always a stated feature of the PDC, you will also need to check and know the vehicle's dimensions – height, width and length. Finally, you should also make sure that you feel fit and well enough before driving.

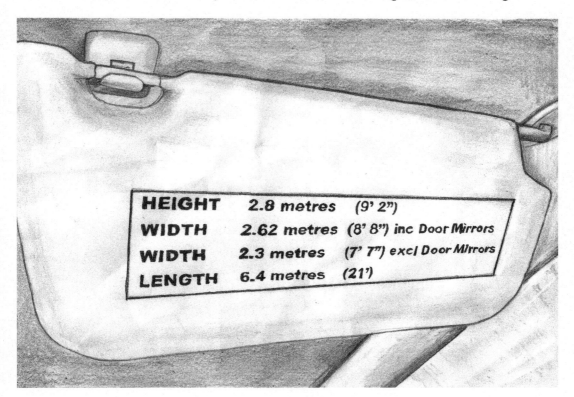

HEIGHT	2.8 metres	(9' 2")
WIDTH	2.62 metres	(8' 8") inc Door Mirrors
WIDTH	2.3 metres	(7' 7") excl Door Mirrors
LENGTH	6.4 metres	(21')

Learning outcomes, with training ...

Emergency Response drivers need to be able to:

- Demonstrate the Pre-Driving Checks (Cockpit drill) on a range of vehicles
- State briefly the reasons and legal requirements for making of the listed checks, particularly the static and mobile brake check.

Chapter 4

VEHICLE OPERATING AND SAFETY SYSTEMS

Vehicle operating and safety systems will vary according to the purpose it is being used for. Standard active or passive safety features can be detected when switching on the dashboard warning lights. These should in any case be checked as part of the Pre-Driving Check (PDC) for any warning of malfunction.

Vehicle safety systems are no replacement for responsible driving or proper training. The best and most effective protection against collisions is to drive in a style that prevents them.

Some common operating features on response vehicles include:

1. Emergency lights control. Supplied by Carnation Designs (Includes "Genisys^{TM} ")

2. Battery isolator switches

3. Electrical charge support system

4. Reversing camera

5. Run-lock

Run-lock allows the driver to leave the vehicle engine running with the ignition keys removed and the vehicle securely locked. Due to the high current consumption of ancillary equipment, including blue lights, and ancillary lighting used at the scene this can be necessary when attending roadside calls for long periods. If the vehicle is entered unlawfully for the purpose of theft, once any of the inputs have been triggered, such as handbrake release, this will cut the engine and will not restart without the ignition key.

Other electronic features that may be available as standard can include adaptive cruise control and tyre pressure monitoring. Some vehicles may also be equipped with a fire extinguisher.

Vehicle safety systems are designed to:

1. Actively help drivers avoid a collision by staying in control. Known as Actively Safety systems, these use automated devices that intervene before a crash occurs in an attempt to prevent it happening. For instance, Anti-lock Brakes (ABS). This prevents the wheels from locking up when the driver brakes, enabling the driver to steer while braking. Traction control

(TC). This prevents the wheels from slipping while the car is accelerating. Electronic Stability Control (ESC). This works by monitoring the lateral movement of the car and before a driver can detect a skid is happening, it applies the brakes to individual wheels. Emergency Brake Assist (EBA) applies firmer pressure.

2. Passively protect and prevent injuries where the collision is unavoidable. Passive safety systems include features that help to protect occupants during a crash. These include airbags, seat-belts, head restraints, crumple zones, collapsible steering columns, side-impact and anti-roll bars.

Learning outcomes with training

Emergency response drivers will know and comply with:

- Organisational safety and maintenance policy

Emergency response drivers will be able to state the use and effects of

- Active vehicle safety systems
- Passive vehicle safety systems

Emergency response drivers will be able to state briefly how the following vehicle safety systems work:

- Anti-lock Brakes (ABS)
- Traction control (TC)
- Electronic Stability Control (ESC).

Emergency response drivers will:

- Know the limitations of safety aids such as the reversing camera
- Be familiar with the types of emergency lights panel fitted to a variety of vehicles
- Check that any electrical charge support system is disconnected before driving
- Know when and how to use run-lock

Chapter 5

NAVIGATING DIRECTIONS - GLOBAL SATELLITE POSITIONING AND THE ROAD ATLAS

GPS satellite navigation systems

SatNav systems are relied upon to direct us accurately to the correct destination.

We run the risk of trusting our satellite navigation systems far too much, meaning that we think less for ourselves. We are driving, not the SatNav. We can't blame this device if we have a collision or commit an offence.

Destination planning should normally be done before starting to drive, checking preferences, such as whether the fastest or shortest route is best, or whether to avoid motorways or not. If the SatNav has to be re-programmed on the move, to avoid distraction, this needs to be done by the co-driver or crew member. Otherwise, pull over.

If the SatNav is fixed to the window, it should be in the driver's line of sight, but must not block the view of the road. We don't want to have to look down or turn the head too much.

When taking directions we must trust our own eyes, and not the SatNav. We should listen to receive spoken instructions and only glance at the screen. Observe all traffic signs and if the road looks wrong, don't take it.

We know the type of vehicle we are driving, the SatNav probably doesn't. We can never be sure that a road is suitable for our vehicle because the SatNav has told us to go down it. Watch particularly for height and width warning signs.

MapCraft Skills

Because there is always some risk of the navigation system failing, response drivers, and co-drivers need to have map reading skills. A hard copy map of the local area or regional road atlas needs to be kept in the vehicle.

SatNav devices need regular updates for new roads or traffic systems. Various mobile apps may also be useful tools to assist directional information; however these can only be operated by the co-driver or another crew member, and again, may have limitations. No electronic system, or hard copy can be expected to always be fully up to date or perfect, so be ready to deal with errors.

Local knowledge develops with practical driving experience. Having mentorship with a crew member who is familiar with the area will be a real practical benefit.

Response drivers, with training will be able to:

1. Use navigational aids safely during routine driving and when responding to emergency calls

2. Overcome any limitations of navigation aids, including Mobile Data Terminal (MDT) system

3. Use navigational aids safely to assist in routine driving and an emergency response

4. Give directional information to the driver

5. Take directional information from the co-driver or another crew member

6. Manage distractions from within the vehicle during routine driving and when responding to emergency calls.

Chapter 6

DRIVING PLANS

For the professional driver, things do not just happen.

With adequate concentration and proper observation, there's normally enough time to recognise a danger and respond early and appropriately. Nothing on the road ever happens 'suddenly'.

The majority of driving situations are predictable and can be read. The observation links and clues are there for the driver who is planning ahead.

Driving plans are a 'must'. Everything in this chapter is a consideration that contributes towards your driving plan(s). The essential parts of the planning process involve:

- Hazard Perception - Anticipating actual or potential danger
- Prioritising those hazards presenting the greatest risk
- Deciding what to do

HAZARD PERCEPTION, AWARENESS AND ANTICIPATION

Hazard perception is an important part of learning to drive. To achieve a mastery of traffic situations response, drivers need to be ready for all developing hazards, throughout the journey. Awareness and anticipation improves with driving experience and the amount of effort you put into improving it.

A very common example is driving behind the vehicle in front, particularly if it is a heavy goods vehicle. By dropping back two or three vehicle lengths, not only will the view be increased, but the overall stopping distance will be improved.

Deciding what to do in any situation is the main feature of any driving plan. Decisions can be drawn from the predictability of other road users behaviour. Your plan needs to be based on:

a) What you can see
b) What you can't see
c) What you can reasonably expect to happen

Typically, a driving plan prioritises the greatest risk, from all that can be seen in front, to the sides and behind. A contingency "Plan B" may be needed to deal with b) and c). Some instructors call this having an "escape route".

A good driving plan will keep you:

1. In the correct road position
2. Travelling at the correct speed
3. With the correct gear selected

Keep asking yourself what you will do if things change. Constantly, that is every three to five seconds, update the information.

Your driving instructor will show you how to put the changing information into a driving plan using "The System of Vehicle Control", often affectionately known as "The System".

Learning outcomes, with training …

Emergency response drivers will be able to:

- Demonstrate a driving plan using concentration, observation and prioritising the most serious hazard(s)
- Demonstrate adaptability where things turn out differently, that is, having a Plan B as a contingency
- Make and carry out practical driving decisions, without hesitation, in a methodical manner

Emergency response drivers will be able to demonstrate:

- Situational awareness
- Visual scanning technique

Emergency response drivers will be able to identify:

- Primary hazards
- Secondary hazards

1. THE SYSTEM OF VEHICLE CONTROL

The purpose of "the system" is to prevent collisions by providing an approach to traffic and road hazards that is safe, systematic, simple and is applicable in all circumstances.

Driver error is the cause of most crashes. Having a systematic approach to all hazards minimizes the risk of a blameworthy collision considerably.

The "system" originated in the early 1930s, designed by racing drivers to reduce the high number of police vehicle collisions occurring at the time. Since the middle of the 1950s, the system has become the bench mark for all advanced driver training.

In 1988 a "National Working Party" was set up by the Government's Home Office to review whether "Roadcraft techniques" were still fit for purpose. After six years of thorough investigation, the "System" proved itself to still be the best/safest method of driving for all on-road driving. In 1994, a new style "Roadcraft" was launched. It is reviewed every year by "The Roadcraft Reflective Practitioners Group" to ensure that it never becomes out of date. We can safely say that today, the "system" provides the up-to-date driving competencies necessary to master everyday traffic situations.

Adopting the system does not mean that you will never be involved in a collision, just that you should not be blameworthy.

Three hazard types

Throughout each of the phases of the system, the driver processes and prioritises "information"- taking, using and giving. This is made very easy by dividing hazards into three types; these being:

- **Fixed / physical features,** such as junctions, bends, pedestrian crossings etc.

- **Moving features.** Developing hazards, specifically all other road users

- **Environmental features.** Such as how road surfaces are affected by the weather.

The phases of "The System"

Driving instructors often use the mnemonic "**IPSGA**" when coaching the system. This will help you remember these phases:

- **Information** – processed correctly throughout each phase keeps your vehicle both safe and stable

1. **Position** – for the intended course to travel ahead, change lane or to turn. Before changing this, the appropriate mirror(s) need to be checked and a signal considered

2. **Speed** – You must be able to pull up in the distance seen to be clear. On rural roads this is the distance between you and the limit (vanishing) point of your visibility. Often, speed can be lost through deceleration, otherwise braking is needed. This should be while the vehicle is travelling straight and there should only be one piece of (primary) braking.

    Before reducing speed, use the mirror(s). When braking, your brake lights will be a signal that you are slowing.

3. **Gear** – Once deceleration and/or braking is complete, the correct gear to negotiate the hazard should be selected. Use the brakes to slow; then select the correct gear to go. Ideally there should be no overlap of braking and gear changing, keeping engine revs sustained as the clutch is smoothly and fully re-engaged. Keep a check on any following vehicles, or those to the side, by using the mirrors fully.

4. **Acceleration** – normally lightly into the hazard, then more positively. Always smoothly. Continue to use the mirrors so that you are always aware of the movements of traffic to your side and rear.

Applying these phases correctly, continuously assessing "information" will ensure safe and smooth passage through the hazard. Who could want anything less?

Learning outcomes, with training ...

Emergency response drivers will be able to:

- Describe the phases of the system of vehicle control
- Demonstrate the phases of vehicle control in their correct sequence
- Describe the term "hazard" and the three main types
- Demonstrate ability to identify hazards
- Apply the system of vehicle control at different types of hazards
- Demonstrate ability to prioritise which hazards present the greatest risk
- Recognise and use limit points correctly.

Emergency response drivers will be able to negotiate:

- Fixed hazards (eg road layout)
- Dynamic hazards (moving vehicles)
- Environmental hazards (weather)

Emergency response drivers will be able to demonstrate:

- Systematic driving

2. OBSERVATION AND ANTICIPATION TECHNIQUES

Of the five human senses, observation is the most important for driving. Information that can be seen needs to be interpreted accurately, for instance on a National Speed Limit road, the severity of a bend ahead. Early observations will provide more time to respond correctly.

When driving at high speeds, accurate perception is also particularly important. The optical illusion below gives an example of a misinterpretation of information where the bottom line appears longer than the top line. Measure both lines, they are the same length.

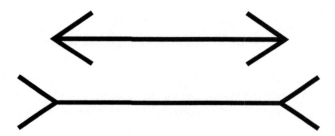

Looking but not seeing

Quite often, drivers only see what they expect to see when they need to take action. This usually results in driving actions being late and subsequently rushed.

'Failure to look properly' is the most common contributory factor recorded for most road traffic collisions. Other factors include 'failure to judge another person's path or speed', 'carelessness or recklessness', or 'judged to be in a hurry'.

In the words of former World Motor Racing Champion, Jackie Stewart - "Seeing is not something that happens, seeing is something you do."

Scanning the environment – where to look

Most driving mistakes are caused by bad habits in the way drivers use, or rather don't use their eyes. The vision available is:

- Central vision - ahead
- Peripheral vision
- Side and rear vision using the mirrors

Emergency response drivers will rapidy scan the whole road environment. In the central vision ahead, scanning the far distance, the middle distance and the immediate foreground is extremely important. Peripheral vision helps us detect events to the side that are important, even when we're not looking directly at them. The mirrors need to be used effectively to know what is to the side or behind our vehicle. Quick side glances can also be essential before changing position or turning.

During training, your driving instructor will need to be sure that you have an ability to notice many things at once in routine driving, before beginning the emergency response element. Important judgments like estimating the speed and distance of other traffic is critical to safe and defensive driving. A way to enhance driving to "The System" is to scan the road using the five good driving habits, known as the "Smith System":

1. **Look well ahead** – the far, as well as the middle distance
2. **Move your eyes** – use the mirrors and check your peripheral vision
3. **Spot the problems** – prioritise the hazards
4. **Keep space** – maintain a space cushion and keep an escape route
5. **Be seen** – use your headlights, signals and if necessary, your horn

Learning to scan effectively may take a little time, depending on your previous learning experience and also your own commitment to developing awareness.

Zones of visibility

Each road has different zones of vision. For example, emerging at a traffic junction, where you need to check each zone before proceeding.

In all cases, where vision is restricted we need to get as much information as we can, such as:

- Coming up to a rural bend, look for breaks in hedgerows, fences and walls
- Approaching an urban corner, use the reflection in shop windows as a mirror to see any approaching traffic
- At night, the angle of other vehicle's headlights or taillights can show the curvature of the road ahead

Observation - Information and action links

Think – what will happen next, for instance where you see:

- Passengers are beginning to stand up on a bus
- An ice cream van parked at the roadside
- Stationary vehicles in a lay-by
- Vehicle movement in or around a fuel station

The level of risk with potential or actual danger associated with hazards will vary according to:

- The hazard itself
- How close it is to you
- The road layout
- Whether the hazard is moving or not
- How fast you are approaching it

Learning outcomes, with training ...

Response drivers will develop observation skill by:

- Moving the eyes and looking in all directions
- Looking for hazards of any shape and size and from all directions
- Demonstrating how information is used while driving
- Judging the level of third party error

3. THE IMPORTANCE OF TRAFFIC SIGNS AND ROAD MARKINGS

Traffic signs and road markings convey messages. Depending on the type of sign you see; it will direct, inform or control the behaviour of road users. As well as the hazards you can meet on the road, traffic signs tell you the rules that you must obey. Road markings have a similar role. They are rather like punctuation marks in text, they help you to read the road.

All emergency response drivers need to have an up to date and thorough knowledge of traffic signs and road markings. You need to observe all signs early enough to understand their meaning and act safely in response.

To stress the importance of traffic signs, the written tests for blue-light ambulance drivers demand a full and comprehensive knowledge of each definition of all published signs. The pass mark for each examination is 100%.

The 'Highway Code' and 'Know Your Traffic Signs' contain all the technical detail that you need.

Learning outcomes, with training ...

Response drivers will show accuracy of observation by:

- Early identification of all traffic signs and road markings
- Recognising the relevance of traffic signs and road markings
- Give examples of traffic signs that give:
  - orders
  - warn
  - information

Response drivers will be able to state:

- The exact definitions of the most common traffic signs

4. EFFECTIVE USE OF ALL MIRRORS

When applying the system of vehicle control, the response driver needs to always be aware of what is travelling at the rear and at each side of the vehicle, as well as what is going on up ahead.

Drivers must be fully aware of how different types of mirror (flat and convex glass) can affect our perception of how far away other vehicles actually are.

- Flat mirrors give an accurate image of the road behind, making it easier to judge the speed and distance of following traffic

- Convex mirrors give a wider field of view. This means that any vehicle behind seems smaller and could be closer than you think.

All mirrors must be set correctly as a critical part of the pre-driving checks. A full offside blind-spot check is essential, only before moving off from the roadside.

Offside blind-spot checks while on the move should not be necessary. This is because your eyes will be off the road ahead and can be dangerous, especially when driving at high speeds. To cover any blind areas when changing lanes, joining motorways or dual carriageways from a slip road, or before manoeuvring where traffic is merging from the left or right, a quick sideways glance is an acceptable alternative and in some circumstances, encouraged.

Learning outcomes, with training ...

Response drivers will demonstrate the appropriate mirrors on all critical occasions, including well before:

- Moving off and stopping – from roadside and in stop-start traffic
- Changing direction, including lanes
- Changing speed
- Giving a direction signal

5. USE OF SIGNALS TO COMMUNICATE CLEARLY

Signals are our means of communication with all other road users. They need to be given in a timely manner, where they help warn or inform another road user of your presence or intention.

Range of signals

We can ensure clear and unmistakable communication using:

- Direction indicators
- Brake lights
- Horn
- Hazard warning lights
- Headlights
- Arm signals
- Courtesy hand signals

Making the best use of one, or a combination of these methods of signaling requires an early assessment of the circumstances along with a use of the mirrors before signaling.

The need for a signal should be considered:

- When dealing with a hazard, that requires a change of direction or speed
- Whenever it would benefit another road user

Avoid any confusion, by ensuring that your signals are not misleading, for example:

- Signaling when passing parked vehicles or a moving pedal cyclist, is usually unnecessary, particularly if you applying the system by adopting the correct road position early. An unnecessary right turn signal may suggest to other road users that you intend to make a right turn

- If you intend to pull up just beyond a junction on the left, do not indicate before the junction. Another road user might believe that you are going to turn into that junction

- Ensure that you cancel the indicator as soon as your manoeuvre has been completed

Use of direction signals state an intention and do not give a right to carry out a manoeuvre.

Take care not to accept an indicator as a guarantee of another road user's intentions; look for supporting evidence such as a marked reduction in the speed of the vehicle.

Be cautious how you interpret other's signals, for instance:

- Where another driver flashes the headlights. Are you sure of the driver's intentions? Before you proceed, consider whether the signal was meant for you.

Use of the horn

The horn is a signal. Sound only where it could benefit other road users, particularly where they are unaware of your presence:

- Before sounding the horn make sure that, if the horn is not heard, your speed is such that you can stop the vehicle in plenty of time

- Use the horn in good time

- Adjust the length of the note to suit the circumstances, that is, a short note to a pedestrian in view, but a longer note when dealing with a hump bridge having restricted space and vision

Flashing Headlights

Headlight flashes should only be used where the horn would not be heard, and in place of the horn at night as a warning of your presence:

- Never assume that a headlight flash from another driver is a signal to proceed. Assess the situation carefully

- If you need to warn another road user in front of your intention to overtake in daylight, use a three second flash of your headlights early to give them plenty of warning and to avoid dazzle. Take care not to confuse any other road user or appear aggressive when you do this

- At night, consider a three second headlight flash when approaching a hill crest, narrow hump bridge or when travelling along a narrow winding road

Brake Light Signals

These indicate your intention to slow down or stop. If a driver is travelling too close behind you, a light touch on the foot brake in advance of the hazard will provide an alert of your driving plan.

Rear fog lights

These are much brighter than brake lights and therefore may mask them when you are slowing down. Only use where visibility is seriously reduced, that is to less than 100 metres.

Arm Signals

These are still stated on the Highway Code. Because they are no longer in regular use, if given correctly other road users are more likely to take notice of them. Arm signals must not be used when both hands are needed on the steering wheel.

Courtesy Hand Signals

Acknowledging courtesy on the road demonstrates a positive attitude, encourages good driving, and promotes courtesy and consideration. Do use courtesy signals to:

- Thank another road user

- Apologise when you have unintentionally caused inconvenience

A courtesy signal can be given, such as by raising your left hand towards the approaching driver. This can also be done without taking your hand off the wheel by simply raising the palm of your hand or nodding your head. As an alternative, your attendant may do it for you.

- Do not signal another road user to make a manoeuvre, this could be dangerous. Hold back where necessary and only proceed when safe

Learning outcomes, with training ...

Response drivers need to demonstrate the clear use of all signals. This means giving signals:

- Where necessary
- In plenty of time
- Correctly

6. ROAD POSITION

Correct road position will assist the response driver's progress through traffic. On emergency response, a "position of strength" is a dominant position where, in effect we manage the traffic in front. Other drivers will see our road position as an indication of our intended course, that is, where we intend to go.

In both routine and response driving, establishing a road position, such as approaching a bend that improves what we can see and enables our vehicle to be seen will assist our progressive driving. A position that facilitates 'early vision, early decision' will assist safe progress.' When driving on emergency response, early use of an extended road position allows a lot of the work to be done for us in clearing other vehicles.

There will be times when we will need to retire to a "position of safety" due to the actions or movements of other road users. Your driving instructor will illustrate and guide you on these aspects as they occur during training. Overall choice of road position depends on a number of things, including:

1. Safety – this is the overriding factor
2. Routine or emergency response driving
3. Observation
4. Road layout
5. Traffic conditions
6. Assisting traffic flow
7. Cornering
8. Manoeuvrability
9. Making our intentions clear

General risk assessments

1. Nearside
   - Parked vehicles and their occupants. Allow at least an open door's width

- Pedal cyclists. Allow as much room as you would when overtaking a car
- Pedestrians. Check all pedestrian movements. Give them plenty of room

2. Offside

- Avoid potential conflict with approaching traffic. Keep to the left and reduce speed if necessary.

Where the road narrows and there are risks on both nearside and offside, safe progress may be possible by adopting a mid-line road position, reducing speed if necessary.

3. Positioning for visibility

- Your view into nearside junctions can be improved by positioning towards the crown of the road. This also has the benefit of allowing other road users to see you.

4. Following position

The advantages of maintaining an adequate following distance are:

- A better view of the road ahead. To improve the view on both sides of the vehicle, minor adjustments to the left or right can assist observation of what is happening in the road ahead
- You will be able to better judge when to move up into an overtaking position
- You will be able to stop your vehicle, should the driver in front brake firmly without warning
- You can increase your braking distance so that the driver behind will have more time to react

5. Position for overtaking

- Where you identify an opportunity to overtake, you can prepare by moving up closer to the target vehicle.
- Avoid intimidating the other driver or appearing aggressive. This can be both dangerous and counter-productive. If the other driver speeds up, it will make the overtake difficult.

6. Stopping positions

When pulling up behind other vehicles in traffic queues, consider:

- A minimum gap of about one car length

This is better than simply seeing the "tyres and tarmac" as it provides more of an escape route if the driver in front experiences a difficulty moving off. Also:

- If you are shunted from the back there is less risk of collision with the vehicle in front.
- If you receive a response call, the driver in front is less likely to panic and over-react

When stopping near a bend on rural roads, stop on the bend rather than round the bend. This will allow following traffic more time to see you, giving them more time to slow down

7. Parking

When parking facing uphill, consider leaving the vehicle:

- In a low forward gear and turn the steering wheels away the kerb-edge

When parking facing downhill, consider leaving the vehicle:

- In reverse gear and turn the steering wheels towards the kerb-edge

Learning outcomes, with training …

Emergency Response drivers will be able to demonstrate the principles of correct positioning of the vehicle according to varying road and traffic conditions, in both routine and response driving.

Emergency Response drivers will be able to state briefly, the common factors to be risk assessed when deciding:

- The correct line for left and right hand bends

- What factors influence the margin to be allowed with the vehicle in front in varying traffic situations on urban / rural roads / multi-lane roads including motorways

7. SPEED AND STOPPING DISTANCES

The public perception of response vehicles is that they drive not only quickly, but fast. When responding to an emergency, your choice of speed has to be appropriate for the circumstances. When you double your speed, you quadruple your stopping distance.

You must always be able to stop safely in the distance seen to be clear, on our side of the road, without inconveniencing other road users. This rule applies to all road types but must be 'halved' when driving on single track or three-quarter width (narrower) roads. Essentially we're making that allowance for the hypothetical 'other' vehicle coming towards.

Your first consideration has to be whether you are competent to drive at speed. Are there any human factors, such as fatigue, or stress that mean that you shouldn't be driving at high speeds? If you are all good; then are you are familiar with the controls and handling characteristics of the vehicle that you'll be driving?

Speed-choice, particularly when driving a fast-response car on urban roads, through shopping and residential areas must be safe. It is very easy to underestimate the car's road speed, so check your speedometer regularly. An error can be disastrous.

Learning outcomes, with training …

Emergency Response drivers will always:

- Drive at an appropriate speed for the road, traffic and weather conditions

When responding to an emergency call, response drivers will always:

- Drive at an acceptable speed within Service Policy Guidelines

Emergency Response drivers will know the speed limits of:

- The vehicle being driven
- All classes of vehicle, such as lorries, buses and those that are towing

Emergency Response drivers will know and apply the correct following distances:

- On all types of road surfaces
- In all kinds of weather conditions
- At all speeds, including those over 70mph

8. OVERTAKING MOVING TRAFFIC

This is one of the most hazardous manoeuvres you can perform, primarily because it is the most likely to bring you into conflict with other road users.

On most National Speed Limit (NSL) routes single carriageways, overtaking is effectively discouraged because of the continuous long curves and restricted visibility. Restrictions are also engineered, for instance traffic islands, cross-hatching and the use of solid white lines in the centre of the road.

Where overtaking is possible risk is minimised with a good assessment of speed and distance of other traffic. The stretch of road needs to be safe and the anticipated overtake needs to be performed quickly.

Driving instructors may offer varying ways of using overtaking techniques. Examples are "box-overtaking" or "the rule of the triangle". You can expect to be taken onto suitable NSL roads and be given guidance on "friendly follow" of the target vehicle, "holding back" until an overtaking opportunity presents itself. At the discretion of the course director, staged overtakes with training vehicles may be permitted.

In all instances, manage the risks by asking yourself these questions:

- Is the overtake necessary?
- Is your vehicle capable of the manoeuvre?
- Has the driver in front seen you?
- Is the driver being obstructive?
- Can you see far enough ahead to be sure it is safe?
- Will you come into conflict with any other road user – the closing gap?
- Will you cause any other vehicle to alter course or speed?
- Will you be able to avoid creating a third line of vehicles abreast?
- Will you be able to move back to the nearside in plenty of time?
- Can you abort the overtake should another hazard present itself?

Prior to overtaking, we need to take into account:

- Other vehicles in front and behind
- Road surface layout and conditions
- Whether to overtake more than one vehicle
- Type of road – such as single carriageway
- Whether approaching a junction or bend
- Vehicles in lay-bys
- The likelihood of roadworks
- Risks associated by following another overtaking vehicle

1. Non-response – Overtaking

With the assistance of your instructor, adapt the flexible features of the system to the planned overtake. Check rear view and side mirrors between each phase and consider a signal (this could be a three second headlight flash) before commencing movement into the final overtaking position.

Information

Initial Scenario:

- Rural environment (Country road)
- National Speed Limit applies on single carriageway (two-way) road ahead
- White hazard lines, changing to centre lines on a straight road into the far distance
- No other hazards identified
- You are catching up with a single moving vehicle ahead that is travelling more slowly; this is selected as a target vehicle for overtake.

Observe for changes to this scenario, such as one or more new approaching vehicles; look for the development and appearance of a suitable gap. In anticipation of such a gap, select the best gear for acceleration.

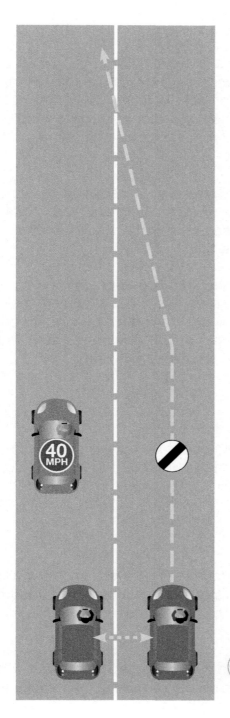

Overtaking on a single carriageway road

Position

Avoid being too close to the target vehicle. Having caught up and matched your speed and gear to the slower moving target vehicle, choose a suitable following road position, suited for best visibility. This first position should enable you, by very slight movements of your steering to keep the best view of the road ahead. Your instructor may also include reference to the vision down the target vehicle's nearside.

Dependent on visibility and safety ahead, your instructor will coach you when to begin positioning the outside wheels over the centre white line, before positioning fully over to the offside of the carriageway (all wheels over); prior to any full commitment to the overtake.

"Position for vision" when able and "position for safety" when not. Because we position the vehicle in this way, it means that we do not necessarily commit to the overtake. It does afford us the vision to see and make an informed decision, keeping the escape route option open. That is, to return to the previous following position on the left.

Speed

The Highway Code advises drivers to "move quickly past the vehicle you are overtaking". Your range of speed will be limited to the road conditions and the maximum speed for your vehicle.

Gear (Manual box)

When the gap has been identified (during the Position phase) you should select a lower gear. The selection of this gear will not only give good deceleration qualities if speed needs to be reduced, but is also the most responsive to carry out the overtake quickly.

If you are driving a vehicle with an automatic gearbox, select "Sports" mode and/or use "Kick-down". (You can easily check the manufacturers advice on these features with an internet search).

Acceleration

Accelerate keeping both hands on wheel. Once you have passed the target vehicle safely, adjust the speed as necessary. Use the nearside and interior mirrors to help determine when it will be safe to return to the left. No indicator / direction signal is required or expected at this stage, as you are returning to your normal road position on the left. The engine can then be rested by selecting a higher gear, appropriate to the road speed.

2. Emergency response - Overtaking

Whether you are in an urban or rural environment, maintain a driving plan and use the system.

Before overtaking we are looking for driver's ahead showing the "moment of realisation", when they have become aware that we are following behind. To identify this, from the list below, we are looking for at least two signs of their use of mirrors.

- Brake lights activated
- Visible reduction in speed
- Indicates an intention to move left
- The vehicle physically moves left

When overtaking lines of traffic, our driving plan needs to include observation for any vehicle signalling an intention to turn right. We must reduce speed, anticipating that the vehicle might turn. Consider use of the bull horn.

Learning outcomes, with training ...

Emergency response drivers will:

- Apply the system to overtaking manoeuvres in both response and non-response situations

- Identify safe opportunities for overtaking on a blue-light call
- Pass other vehicles safely while on a blue-light call
- Exercise patience and keep on the side of safety
- Be able to justify any exemptions claimed while overtaking on response

Emergency response drivers will know:

- The four occasions when it may be permissible to overtake on the left
- Occasions when a driver MUST NOT overtake
- The vehicle performance capabilities that influence a decision to overtake.

9. URBAN ROADS

Depending on the time of day, urban roads can carry considerable traffic. Many different people use the roads, all going about their business.

Because there are various distractions that reduce attention, the response driver has to think for other road users. A balancing has to be achieved between making progress, with being cautious.

Considerations include our anticipation of not only car drivers, but also:

*   Bus, lorry and motorcyclists

Dealing with vulnerable road users, namely:

*   Pedestrians, especially children
*   Pedal cyclists.

Observation is the main component of anticipation. Things do not just happen randomly, situations normally develop. Anticipation is the ability to identify, particularly developing hazards at the earliest opportunity.

In an unfamiliar town, to assist observation, road layouts are normally signposted, and there may be other clues if you are able to look far enough ahead. Familiar roads may seem easier, but beware of the dangers of driving on memory rather than sight. Things have a habit of changing.

Determining accurately what other road users are going to do usually improves with experience behind the wheel. In some instances, such as at junctions, making eye-contact can be a useful way of ensuring safety.

Urban observation and action links. For instance:

Observation :   Line of parked vehicles

Action: Expect doors opening, vehicles moving off, pedestrians, including children stepping out

Observation: Service bus

Action: Expect bus driver to serve stops

Observation: Pedestrian hailing a taxi cab

Action: Taxi driver will respond to the potential fare

Learning outcomes, with training ...

Emergency response drivers will, in the urban environment be able to demonstrate:

- Concentration
- Observation
- Awareness and anticipation
- Effective driving plans to suit developing hazards
- Application of the system to all urban hazards

10. RURAL ROADS

When we look at the country's casualty statistics, around 60% of traffic collision fatalities happen on country roads.

Country roads often have:

- Sharp bends. Slow before the bend, do not brake in it
- Hidden dips (dead ground)
- Concealed farm and building entrances
- Horse riders. They may ride in double file when escorting a young or inexperienced horse or rider.
- Slow moving farm vehicles such as tractors
- Livestock / wild animals.

Where the road surface is wet or slippery, such as when there is mud, speed needs to be reduced. Especially in the summer, overgrown verges, bushes and trees can block your view and potentially obscure an oncoming hazard. Again, your speed needs to be correct.

The speed limit is a limit not a target. On national speed limit single carriageways, the average free flow speed is 48mph. This speed will not be safe when passing more vulnerable road users such as horse riders, cyclists and walkers. Pass wide and slow.

The best practical way to make the best speed-choice is use the "limit point" of your visibility. This being the furthest point you can see ahead. Also known as the 'vanishing point', it is the last and furthest point ahead, where the roadside edges converge. It is the point where the road surface 'disappears' around the bend.

As you approach each limit point, the view ahead can open up away from you, or it may get closer, in which case, speed must be reduced and if the bend is sharp, the horn should be considered.

Familiarity with country roads can be a danger. Never take it for granted as the conditions can be different every time.

Learning outcomes, with training ...

Emergency response drivers will, in the rural environment be able to demonstrate:

- Concentration
- Observation
- Awareness and anticipation
- Effective driving plans to suit developing hazards
- Application of the system to all rural hazards

11. DIMINISHED VISIBILITY AND AT NIGHT

"Night - the hours of darkness" is defined in law as the period between half an hour after sunset and half an hour before sunrise.

This section relates to not only driving in the hours of darkness, but is relevant to conditions which are less than full daylight, including dawn, as well as dusk. In these conditions, your vision gives you less information.

Some drivers do however feel there are advantages to driving in darkness. For instance, on country roads, you may see the glow of the headlights of approaching vehicles, such as while they are still over the brow of a hill, or coming down side-roads through hedges. The disadvantages include the reduction in contrast, colour and edges, as well as increased difficulty in judging speed and distance of other traffic.

Before we begin any journey, we complete our Vehicle Daily Inspection (VDI):

- All lights are working
- Headlights adjusted to suit the vehicle load
- Clean lenses and indicator lights
- Clean all windows, inside as well as outside (Glare on windows is caused by a film of moisture, grease or dirt)
- All wipers, windscreen washes and demisters checked to be in good working order

Response drivers using familiar urban roads with powerful sodium street lighting may feel quite comfortable driving at night. Extra care is however needed when driving from well-lit to darker areas.

On rural roads at night we can determine the contours of the road ahead by observing the:

- Headlights and taillights of other vehicles
- Cats-eyes and hazard marker posts. The more cats-eyes there are, the greater the danger

Be prepared for road closures and diversions, including on motorways. Repair and maintenance works are often carried out overnight.

We are likely to experience fatigue, particularly in the early hours of the morning. Our awareness and anticipation needs to remain sharp, especially when dealing with vulnerable road users such as pedestrians and pedal cyclists, who may well also be tired or possibly inebriated. Should you feel fatigue, pull over in a suitable place, get some fresh air, rest and if possible, get some refreshments before continuing your journey.

We can be dazzled not only by the main beam headlights of approaching drivers, but also by the brake or fog lights of the vehicle in front. As with approaching headlights, look away from them. You may also need to slow down and hold back. Take care not be distracted by reflections inside and outside the vehicle.

The law states the minimum lighting requirements. You are only required to drive on sidelights at night in a built up area. In practice you would use dipped headlights. Outside built up areas you must use dipped headlights. You can use full beam, providing you don't dazzle anyone else. Headlights are a must, when visibility is seriously reduced. Fog lights must only be used where visibility is 100 metres or less.

When parking at night, your vehicle must not face against the direction of the traffic flow unless in a recognised parking space. In a built-up area you must not park within 10 metres (32 feet) away of any junction. Where the speed limit is greater than 30mph, all vehicles must display parking lights.

If you have to park on the road in fog, you must leave your parking lights or sidelights on.

Learning outcomes, with training ...

Response drivers will be able to demonstrate:

- A full Vehicle Daily Inspection
- A system drive during the hours of darkness

- A driving plan for driving on urban roads at night
- A driving plan for driving on rural roads at night
- Correct use of main beam and dipped headlights at night

Emergency response drivers will know:

- The legal definition of the hours of darkness
- The advantages and disadvantages of driving at night
- How to deal with the effects of fatigue
- How driver's field of vision affects vehicle speed whilst driving during the hours of darkness
- How to deal with dazzle and reflections in the vehicle
- The vehicle lighting requirements, including when parking at night and in fog

12. WEATHER

To look at "weather" in context, it has to be one of the most topical things that we discuss as a nation! Furthermore:

- It is one of the three main types of road hazard, the other two being fixed or moving features
- Being prepared for the journey is one of the aspects of the Goals for Driver Education (GDE) matrix
- When making the Pre-Driving checks (PDC) we need to consider the controls that we need to use, considering the likely weather conditions. Eg headlights and windscreen wipers (Point 8)

Bad weather is often blamed for causing collisions, when the actual cause is bad driving and inexperience.

The weather can impact upon how far we can see and how well our vehicle will perform. Whatever the weather, always drive at a safe speed, which will allow you to stop well within a distance from which you can see.

Learning outcomes, with training ...

Emergency response drivers will be able to demonstrate a knowledge of the effects of adverse conditions on driving by explaining briefly, the procedures for driving in:

- Mist or Fog
- Bright sunshine / Low sun
- Light / heavy rain
- High winds
- Sleet or snow or on ice

Also, dealing with possible combinations of any of the above.

Emergency response drivers will know the importance of:

- Efficient windscreen wipers and washers
- Using the demisters correctly to avoid misting on the windscreen
- Dealing with reflected and distracting light effects from wet roads at night; sun behind the landscape

Emergency response drivers will be able to state:

- Where the risks of micro climates are prominent and the effect of these

13. MOTORWAYS

Motorways carry heavy volumes of traffic between our towns. They are statistically our safest roads, with just 3% of collisions and 4% of fatalities. When something does go wrong, the consequences can be severe due to the high speeds involved.

The main reason that these high-speed roads are so safe is because all the traffic is travelling one direction. Also there's no vehicles turning right across traffic and there's an absence of pedestrians and cyclists.

The three main aspects to motorway driving are joining, driving along and leaving.

1. When joining, access is via a slip road, known as the acceleration lane. Use the system. Drivers do have a legal obligation to give way at the end of the slip. Speed choice must therefore be matched to effective observations; including offside mirror use and sideways glances.

2. When driving along, lane discipline is important. Keep to the nearside in lane one, unless overtaking in lanes two or three. Use the system for overtakes and maintain a safe position behind other vehicles that are in front. Do not stay in any other driver's blind-spot for longer than necessary. Avoid in particular the blind spots of foreign articulated trucks.

3. When leaving, use the system. At normal motorway speeds aim to be in lane one by the half-mile sign and signal left at the 300 yard countdown marker. Reduce speed on the deceleration lane / slip road. Re-adjust your perception for non-motorway speeds.

Throughout the motorway journey, scan the whole environment, as far ahead as you can see, as well as the immediate and close distance. Act on traffic signs and signals displayed on the overhead gantries as well as those on the central reserve. Adjust your speed-choice for changing circumstances. Always maintain safe following distances by applying the two-second rule on dry roads.

The maximum speed limit for cars and motorcycles on motorways is 70mph. For vehicles towing a caravan or trailer, all goods vehicles over 7.5 tonnes and buses or coaches over 12 metres in length, the limit is 60 mph. Those vehicles restricted to 60mph are also not allowed to use the outside lane where there are three or more lanes.

"Smart" motorways are being introduced in England, using technology to manage congestion. On these roads, drivers:

- Must keep within the maximum speed shown on the gantries
- Signs can order drivers to "change lane" or "leave motorway at next exit" (Amber lights also flash from top to bottom)
- Can use the hard shoulder, but only when directed
- Can use the refuge areas for emergencies if there's no hard shoulder

As with existing motorways, drivers must never drive under a red "X" (Red lights flash left to right).

Dual Carriageways. Motorways are a safe type of dual carriageway road. Primary route dual carriageways however, can be the most challenging and are potentially the most dangerous roads we drive on as emergency response drivers.

Where the National Speed Limit applies on dual carriageways, traffic is travelling at motorway speeds without the regulations. This means that anyone can use this class of road including vulnerable road users such as learner drivers, pedal cyclists, horses and pedestrians.

When travelling along a dual carriageway with the priority, junctions can appear with very little or no warning; often at 90 degrees on the older style carriageways. When approaching to cross or join a dual carriageway on emergency response, your instructor's guidance is most likely to switch the blues and twos off unless, or until it is clear to proceed. This minimises the risk of drivers over-reacting or panicking, resulting in rear end shunts. If this happens, you must stop, because you are a factor in the collision. This will inevitably delay your response to the emergency call.

Learning outcomes, with training ...

Emergency response drivers will be able to demonstrate:

- System driving when joining, driving along and leaving motorways
- Lane discipline when non-response driving
- Safe progress, having regard to the high speeds encountered
- Excellent judgement of speed and distances of other traffic

Emergency response drivers will be able to state:

- The classes of road vehicles not allowed to use motorways
- The main dangers of motorway driving
- The purpose of the hard shoulder
- How to use the new "Smart" motorways correctly
- How to adapt to driving in fog on motorways
- How to recognise and use emergency cross-over points
- The precautions to take on elevated sections and bridges
- What to do if a vehicle breaks down

14. ENVIRONMENTALLY FRIENDLY

Non-response driving may fit in this category. Emergency response driving does not, as safety factors will always override economy and environmental considerations.

Having said this, much has been done to make response vehicles environmentally friendly. For instance, vehicle manufacturers have responded to consumer demand by improving the body and engine building process to make it more efficient. At the end of a vehicle's working life it is also more easily recyclable. This is in addition to producing engines that create less of the pollutants that damage the environment.

Our Vehicle Daily Inspection (VDI), as part of the vehicle's maintenance schedule is a contribution to eco-safe driving. Checking the tyres reduces wear and maintains satisfactory fuel consumption. A well maintained vehicle will last a longer time, reducing the number of new vehicles that need to be manufactured.

Our professional driving style should always be smooth. For example avoiding hard acceleration and heavy braking, which increase fuel consumption, using cruise control where fitted helps fuel economy. Maneuvering the vehicle on a warm engine also helps. Using the vehicle's air conditioner and other electrical gadgets only when needed can create fuel savings of up to 10%.

Learning outcomes, with training ...

Emergency response drivers will be able to demonstrate:

- A Vehicle Daily Inspection (VDI) including tyre pressure checks
- A driving style devoid of unnecessary accelerating or braking
- Acceleration sense
- Skilfully applying the brakes to achieve optimum smoothness
- The minimum of gear changes (manual box)

Emergency response drivers will be able to state:

- How to report vehicle maintenance defects
- When to use cruise control, where fitted
- The issues concerning open windows / air conditioning use

Chapter 7

HANDLING SKILLS

Correctly performed, the vehicle Daily Inspection (VDI) and Pre-Driving Checks (PDC) will ensure that the vehicle is safe and ready to be driven. Once we are on the move, control of our vehicle and the safety of ourselves and others ultimately depends on the grip between our tyres and the road surface.

At the start of driver training, you can expect to become accustomed to your vehicle's controls, its acceleration and braking capabilities, as well as its handling characteristics. From then on, the public are dependent on emergency response drivers showing good judgement and correct behaviour when utilising their vehicle handling skills.

1. ACCURATE STEERING CONTROL TECHNIQUE

The PDC for correct seating deportment includes the driver being able to reach the full circumference of the steering wheel. When doing this a driver should place both hands on the steering wheel at the 'ten to two' clock face position; palms on the rim with the thumbs up and relax the arms to allow some bend at the elbows. The intention is to ensure maximum leverage when turning the wheel. It will also help to ensure adequate reach to the majority of the switches.

When driving, both hands need to lightly rest on the steering wheel, unless you need to operate another control. Be ready to tighten the grip where necessary, such as when changing manual gears. The wheel should always be turned smoothly and with accuracy, while the vehicle is moving. Avoid dry steering (turning the steering wheel when stationary) as this puts unnecessary wear on the tyres and steering mechanism.

The most widely adopted and preferred steering technique, in the UK, for professionals is the 'pull-push' method. This is not a natural way to steer and needs to be learnt. Used correctly it will give you measured steering that will be accurate.

When turning the wheel, both hands remain on the wheel with the hands level and mirroring each other, one hand grips and makes the turn by pulling or pushing. To make a full turn, one hand leads for the initial pull, beginning from the twelve o' clock position. With this method, the entire wheel is used for full turns and neither hand passes the twelve o'clock or six o'clock position; nor should the steering be allowed to self-centre.

The more natural technique of crossing the hands (rotational steering); arm over arm when steering means that at some point one hand is totally off and away from the wheel; this hand-over-hand technique is considered an unsuitable driving habit for response drivers.   Variations may, however, be considered when manouevring at very slow speeds when using reverse gear or when having to retrieve control during a skid.

However, in the event of a front-end collision, the airbag contained within the steering wheel will inflate at a speed of about 200mph. This immense force is capable of causing severe injury to the driver's arms and face, where the driver is using rotational steering.

Other unacceptable habits that can have an effect on your steering control include resting elbows on the window/door frame or side rests; or having both hands off the wheel at the same time.

Steering modern vehicles is easy as they have power assisted steering (PAS). The system is normally hydraulic, but can be electronic and it assists the driver to turn the wheel. Where graduated PAS is a featured, this means that the slower the vehicle goes the lighter the steering becomes; conversely the faster the vehicle goes the heavier the steering becomes. This is so the driver can 'feel' the tyres on the road.

The two most common steering characteristics are:

1. oversteer (typical of a rear wheel drive vehicle – with the back wheels pushing, the vehicle responds more to steering movements)
2. understeer (typical of a front wheel drive vehicle – with the front wheels pulling, the vehicle responds less to steering movements)

Most skid-training courses will cover these effects in a practical manner.

Learning outcomes, with training …

Emergency response drivers will be able to:

- Maintain and alter the vehicle's direction accurately and with smoothness
- Demonstrate the correct hand position for safe grip with thumbs placed uppermost on the steering wheel
- Turning the steering wheel, using best practice technique advocated for maximum safety and control
- State the factors taken into account to give optimum vehicle control when cornering

2. ACCELERATION SENSE

Acceleration sense is defined in the current Police Drivers' Handbook, Roadcraft, as "the ability to vary vehicle speed in response to changing road speed and traffic conditions by precise use of the accelerator, so that you can use your brakes less or not at all."

In order to use acceleration sense effectively, the driver needs to select the most responsive gear relative to speed-choice, regulating road speed by controlling the accelerator pedal. Some examples of its use are:

1. When moving off

2. Overtaking

3. Complying with speed limits

4. Following other vehicles

5. Negotiating hazards

Effective use depends on:

1. Satisfactory observations

2. Good anticipation

3. Sound judgement of speed and distance

4. Driving experience

5. Vehicle capabilities

Deceleration is where the driver allows the vehicle to slow down using engine compression. The lower the gear the more pronounced the speed reduction.

This will not be so apparent with vehicles fitted with automatic transmission gearboxes, or with diesel engine vehicles. Deceleration is a method of controlling the speed, particularly useful when descending a steep hill or on a slippery road surface. Use care when releasing the accelerator pedal to maintain smoothness.

Poor acceleration sense results in:

- Accelerating away from stationary then having to brake firmly to slow down
- Accelerating up to a slower vehicle then having to brake prior to overtaking
- Falling short of an intending stopping point then having to re-accelerate to reach it

Learning outcomes, with training ...

Emergency response drivers will be able to demonstrate good acceleration sense by:

- Applying the 'acceleration' phase as part of the system of vehicle control
- Knowing the vehicle's acceleration characteristics
- Knowing the vehicle's deceleration characteristics
- Anticipating developing hazards
- Using the accelerator accurately and smoothly
- Maintaining constant speed on a curve
- Use of 'engine braking' to vary vehicle speed in a range of conditions.

Emergency response drivers will be able to:

- State the advantages of using acceleration sense
- Demonstrate when acceleration sense should be applied

3. BRAKING TECHNIQUE

The PDC includes a static and mobile brake check. A static brake check will identify any issues with the hydraulic braking system. If the check is satisfactory, a mobile brake check will confirm that everything is in a safe working order.

Normal use of the brakes has to be gentle and smooth for both slowing and stopping. The technique is often referred to as 'three pressure' or 'tapered braking'. Braking is a three stage process:

1. Takes up the play in the brake pedal
2. Gently increases the pressure as required
3. Slowly relaxes the pressure just before the vehicle stops.

When applying this technique, allowances need to be made for the load or number of passengers being carried, as well as the prevailing road/traffic conditions.   When braking, keep both hands on the steering wheel.

The objective is to keep the vehicle stable. While being driven, a vehicle is at its most stable when it is travelling in a straight line at a constant speed on a level stretch of road with a good surface, so when changing speed or direction we need to ensure that stability remains at a maximum.

Tyre grip on the road is affected by accelerating, braking and steering. Firm braking transfers the vehicle weight to the front wheels and can reduce the ability to steer, as a result:

*   Steering becomes heavier
*   Tyre grip is reduced
*   On a bend it can increase the risk of a loss of control

If you lose vision – lose speed.   Our travelling speed should always be such that we can stop in the distance seen to be clear and on our side of the road. With good reading of the road ahead and proper planning, speed reduction can often be achieved by a period of deceleration before using the brakes, should they be needed at all.

Brakes are for slowing; the gears are for going. With modern dual circuit braking systems, there is no need to use the gears to help slow the vehicle down; also, brakes are cheaper and easier to replace than gear boxes.

Where the system is being used correctly, there should normally only be a single piece of (primary) braking for each hazard. If you habitually need to secondary brake, you are not driving to the system of vehicle control.

Finally, 'comfort braking' is a term sometimes used by instructors to denote a driver's application of the brake where deceleration is sufficient to reduce speed. With practice this habit can be overcome.

Emergency braking

Modern vehicles are equipped with an Anti-Lock Braking System (ABS). The purpose of ABS is to retain steering potential during emergency or harsh braking.

ABS detects the speed at which each wheel is turning and compares this to the pre-programmed data. The system is designed to sense the slowing down of the wheels and to release them before they lock up. It re-applies the brakes once the wheels start to rotate again. Once ABS is activated, the driver has to maintain maximum pressure on the brake pedal throughout. Steering movements are not affected during the operation.

Traction Control (TC) helps prevent wheel spin, such as when the vehicle is starting or accelerating on wet or slippery roads. When spin is detected, the system applies brakes or slows down the engine to regulate spinning and ensure proper contact of tyres.

Emergency Brake Assist (EBA) is fitted to new vehicles. In an emergency situation, EBA increases the pressure. If you brake with force, EBA applies the brakes fully until the ABS kicks in.

Electronic Stability Control (ESC) is designed to assist vehicle stability in an emergency situation. Sensors on each wheel work with a sensor monitoring any rotation (swerving), roll (tilt) or pitch (tip) of the vehicle. A sensor on the steering detects the driver's intended path and can apply the brakes on individual wheels to correct this.

No electronic system is capable of overcoming the laws of physics. The driver is responsible for maintaining full control and keeping the vehicle stable.

Learning outcomes, with training ...

Emergency Response drivers will demonstrate:

- How and when to slow down correctly by easing pressure off of the accelerator
- Skillful application of three pressure (tapered) braking technique when slowing or stopping
- How to use the vehicle's braking system as part of systematic driving, that is correct use of brakes, before any gear is selected.

Emergency Response drivers will be able to explain:

- How and why a static and mobile brake test is carried out
- The considerations for using the brakes, including passenger comfort and vehicle sympathy.

Response drivers will recognise the:

- Type and condition of the road surface – increasing the braking distance In slippery conditions
- Effects of cornering, braking and vehicle balance on the tyre grip.

Emergency Response drivers will know:

- The braking capabilities of the vehicle
- The limits of ABS, Traction Control and Electronic Stability Programmes
- How good the brakes are, but will understand that it is the tyres that produce the grip on the road.

Emergency Response drivers will allow twice the overall stopping distance:

- On wet roads
- On narrow or single track roads. This allows enough room for an oncoming vehicle to also brake.

Emergency Response drivers will allow ten times the overall stopping distance when encountering icy conditions.

4. CHOICE OF GEAR AND TECHNIQUE

In an unfamiliar manual vehicle, before driving, check each gear position. Your instructor can advise you on the best way to grip the lever for effective gear changing.

The gears provide torque (twisting power), this changes engine revolutions into useable power that is transmitted to the road wheels. Skilled gear changing depends on:

- Accurately matching engine and road speed
- Using the clutch and accelerator precisely

Engines typically run between 600 and 6,000 revolutions (revs) per minute (rpm). The manual gearbox enables the driver to alter the ratio of engine rotation relative to that of the road wheels.

Low gears, such as bottom (1st) will provide more power. First gear provides plenty of power but little torque; for instance, when moving off from a stationary position. In slippery road conditions, such as snow or ice, the highest gear possible will be more effective, because this will minimise wheel spin.

Mid-range or intermediate gears are those in between (2nd to 4th or 5th). These gears provide the means of getting to the maximum speed limits quickly, or to maintain a constant speed when climbing a hill. The power available in each intermediate gear, along with the amount of flexibility is dependent on the vehicle. Instructors will advise on this, referring to the manufacturer's handbook where necessary.

Top (6th where fitted) gear will provide more speed. Top gear is a cruising gear, having achieved the maximum speed for a road such as a motorway or National Speed Limit dual carriageway.

When reducing speed, because of the improvements to brake technology, sequential downward gear changes are no longer necessary, and are not acceptable for emergency response driving. "Block" gears changes down are encouraged, missing out unnecessary gears. There may also be times, such as when joining a National Speed Limit dual carriageway where a block change up; for instance, from three to five may be needed.

All gear changes need to be smooth. This reduces wear and tear to the vehicle. It is also beneficial for the stability of the vehicle, as well as for passenger comfort.

Driving to "the system" means that you always have the correct gear selected. This means that you will have the ability to accelerate or decelerate at a moment's notice, for instance, when negotiating corners and bends.

The brakes must be used to slow to the correct speed (not the gears) where deceleration isn't sufficient. Once the vehicle has been slowed sufficiently, then change down to the gear to go. To get this right, the engine revolutions (revs) controlled by the accelerator (gas) pedal should be matched to the gear for the road speed as the clutch is engaged. This is known as "sustained gear changing" (because you are sustaining the engine revs).

There are times, such as when travelling downhill and turning a 90 degree corner (eg a sharp left turn), when braking needs to be continued to maintain the correct speed (not to slow down more) when depressing the clutch and changing down gear.

Some brake/gear overlap therefore may be acceptable, as part of a planned approach; but not as a consequence of approaching a hazard too quickly.

Where a driver overlaps braking and changing gear, there are drawbacks including:

- Only having one hand on the wheel whilst braking
- If not properly controlled it will lead to late and/or excessive braking
- Potentially rushed and jerky gear changes

Coasting, by selecting neutral when slowing or keeping the clutch down, can seriously reduce control of the vehicle. This practice does not save fuel.

Learning outcomes, with training ...

Emergency response drivers will achieve maximum benefit from the manual gearbox by:

- Being in the correct gear for every road speed and traffic situation.
- Making all gear changes quietly and smoothly.
- Being capable of engaging a chosen gear without going through an intermediate gear first.
- Knowing the approximate maximum road speed for each gear of the vehicle. This can be obtained from the manufacturer's handbook.
- Developing good co-ordination between foot and hand.
- Recognising when to change gear by the sound of the engine.
- Choosing the right gear for the speed.
- Using the brakes for slowing and the gears for going (except when descending a hill or where there is a risk of skidding).
- Brake in good time to a speed suitable for negotiating the hazard, then select the correct gear for that speed.
- Matching engine speed to road speed when changing down.
- Not slipping the clutch unnecessarily.
- Not coasting.

Emergency response drivers will be able to state how to:

- Use the gears in a positive, progressive and safe driving style

5. AUTOMATIC GEARBOXES

There is a trend towards most heavy goods vehicles being manufactured with automatic gearboxes. Driving a vehicle fitted with an automatic gearbox has certain advantages, these include:

- Applying more concentration to traffic conditions up ahead.
- Keeping both hands on the wheel for longer periods.

In most cases, with automatic transmission:

- 'P' means 'Park'
- 'R' means 'Reverse'
- 'D' means 'Drive' (Selects all forward gears automatically)

You should:

- Always ensure that the footbrake is applied before engaging 'D' or 'R' when moving away from stationary.
- Do not engage 'D' or 'R' with a high revving engine.

On vehicles with automatic transmission, be aware of the possible "sport" or "lock" options. These provide better road handling. Manual using "lock down" override is a very useful feature when dealing with bends or descending hills.

Learning outcomes, with training ...

Response drivers will demonstrate the correct use of the automatic gear box when:

- Starting the engine
- Routine driving, including short stops
- Driving on an emergency call
- Stopping and leaving the vehicle

Response drivers will know when and how to use:

- The 'kick-down' feature

Response drivers will demonstrate selection and manual use (lock) of the various gears where necessary, such as:

- Travelling downhill
- Dealing with corners and bends

6. DEALING WITH CORNERS AND BENDS

For young drivers, particularly males, there is a high risk of fatality associated with driving round corners and bends. The faster a vehicle is driven, the less tyre grip there will be on the road to maintain stability.

mydriving.co.uk

Limit Point of Visibility

The Limit Point

Safe response driving always requires the driver to be able to stop within the distance you can see to be clear on your own side of the road.   Limit (or vanishing) points are used mainly on the National Speed Limit country lanes as a systematic way of judging the correct speed to use.

The limit point is where the nearside and offside kerb-edges appear to meet. Depending on the corner or bend; as you approach this point, it may move away or towards you. The degree of movement of this point will determine the speed at which the bend can safely be negotiated. If the distance between your vehicle and the limit point decreases, so should the speed; if the distance remains constant so can the speed and if the distance increases consideration can be given to increasing speed. So, the limit point is self-adjusting, allowing you to match your speed to the overall stopping distance.   It also gives you guidance to selecting the correct gear and the acceleration point.

Road camber and surfaces

Most road surfaces are not normally level across their width. To assist drainage, they are often sloped. The slope can help or hinder the vehicle's road-holding depending on how the road bends.

Superelevated curve. For a right hand bend, the best camber will be one that is banked high on the left.   For a left hand bend, the best camber will be one that is banked high to the right. The forces acting upon the vehicle will 'push' the tyres harder onto the road surface, therefore the grip is improved. This type of road is known as being super elevated. imagine driving inside a very large bowl!

Adverse camber. This is where the road surface has the same high banking as the curvature of the road. This type of surface can 'push' you towards the kerb or towards oncoming traffic depending on the direction of the bend. Imagine driving on a very large upside saucer!

Principles of cornering

There are laws of physics associated with any change of direction you make at speed.

A moving vehicle is at its most stable when the driver is accelerating, without increasing speed, in a straight line.

Where a vehicle's speed is increasing, inside the vehicle, you feel as though a force is pushing you back in your seat toward the rear of the car. When changing direction, another force pushes you away from the centre of the curve. In effect, as the driver, or passenger, you feel as though you are being pushed out towards the side of the vehicle.

Your vehicle's stability depends on how much grip your tyres have on the road. Ultimately, this is determined by your observation and forward planning. The three forces you need to control are:

1. Steering

2. Acceleration

3. Braking

Control of our vehicle on corners and bends is maintained by adopting the correct approach, position and speed, and by maintaining pressure on the accelerator pedal. Errors on a left hand bend will risk collision with oncoming traffic. Errors on a right hand bend will take you over the kerb.

The principles of cornering are:

• Correct approach position

• Right choice of speed

• Correct choice of gear

• Maintaining a constant speed through the bend

Correct application of the principles of cornering will achieve a safe, smooth and progressive drive.

Applying the system to corners and bends

Taking a vehicle around a corner or bend is one of our main driving activities. Emergency response courses, therefore, focus on this area, applying the system to ensure you get it right.

Information. This includes:

- Open or closed bend
- The limit point
- The presence of other road users
- The condition of the road surface
- Traffic signs and road markings
- The line of lamp posts, trees, etc.
- Gaps between buildings, fences, etc.
- The angle of headlights at night

Position. For closed bends consider:

- Safety
- Information – observation / view
- Stability - to reduce the tightness of the bend

Where the view on the bend is open, that is clear either side, there may be no worthwhile advantage to changing position.

Positioning for a Left Hand Bend – Towards the centre line, taking into account:

- The width of road and any approaching traffic
- An adverse camber
- How the position of the vehicle might mislead following traffic

Positioning for a Right Hand Bend - Towards the nearside kerb, taking into account:

- The presence of pedestrians
- An adverse camber
- Poor nearside road surface
- Blind junctions, entrances and exits

Speed

The correct speed for the bend will be determined by the

- Limit point
- Condition of the road surface
- Traffic and weather conditions

The degree of movement of the limit point will determine the speed at which the bend can safely be negotiated:

- If the distance between the vehicle and the limit point decreases, so should the speed.
- If the distance remains constant so can the speed.
- If the distance increases consideration can be given to increasing speed.

The limit point is self-adjusting, allowing you to match your speed to the overall stopping distance.   Where brakes are needed, this needs to be one piece of braking with both hands kept on the steering wheel.   If you need to brake on the bend, then you've misjudged it.

Gear

The limit point will also help you determine the correct gear and acceleration points.   Your gear-choice must be the most responsive to the severity of the bend.

Acceleration

As the limit point begins to move away and you begin to straighten the steering, providing there are no other hazards, apply the correct degree of acceleration to leave the bend safely.

It is not how fast you can go round the bend that matters; it is the distance available in which you can stop the vehicle that is important.

Learning outcomes, with training ...

Emergency response drivers will demonstrate the principles of cornering:

- Being capable of being stopped well within the distance you can see to be clear on your own side of the road

Emergency response drivers will demonstrate observation for other dangers and will reduce speed where there are:

- Other dangers, such as potholes caused by wear on the road
- Drainage inspection covers

7. REVERSING, LOW SPEED MANOEUVRING AND USING A BANKSMAN

The majority of collisions while driving at work are when the vehicle is reversing and manoeuvring. This creates the burden of high repair costs, as well as both vehicle and crew downtime.

Where you need to reverse, ensure that a crew member sees you back. This person will take on a banksman's duty. To do this, the person needs to give clear signals by arm and hand, as well as audible commands where these are necessary.

Straight back

Clearance

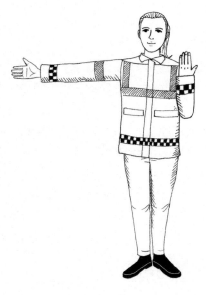

Steer right

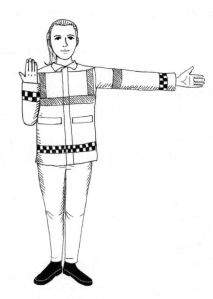

Steer left

STOP!

This means ensuring that the necessary windows are open. The driver retains full responsible for the safety of the vehicle and the manoeuvre.

Always gain agreement with your banksman how and where the parking position will be. The banksman must be in your view, normally the nearside mirror throughout the manoeuvre, should this not be the case then stop the vehicle until you can see them. The banksman must not stand between a moving vehicle and a stationary object.

If you are driving solo, then you need a responsible person to assist you. Be sure that they understand what you are expecting to do.

When reversing or manoeuvring:

- Keep the speed at a very slow walking pace.

- Maintain all round observations, including over your shoulder(s) - not just in the mirrors or using the camera. Watch the front of the vehicle as it swings out to the left or right.

- Turn the steering wheel, only when the vehicle is moving, otherwise damage to the tyres, steering linkage and power assisted steering mechanism is possible.

- Steer accurately. A slow vehicle with fast hand movements may be required in confined spaces.

- Before coming to a halt, where needed, turn the steering wheel ready for the direction of the next vehicle movement.

- In a manual vehicle, avoid over revving the engine against the clutch.

The engine tick over may provide enough power where the road is level.

- In a car, with a clear view through the rear window and reversing in a straight line with minor adjustments, best practice is to place the right hand at the twelve o'clock position to steer and the left arm across the top of the front passenger's seat.

Learning outcomes, with training ...

Emergency response drivers will comply with the Highway Code

- Not reversing further than is reasonably necessary.
- Not reversing from a side road into a main road.

Emergency response drivers will demonstrate the principles of low speed manoeuvring and spatial awareness by:

- Using both forward and reverse gears through a slalom obstacle course

- Bay parking into a garage
- Reverse parking on the left and right sides of the road
- Ensuring correct positioning of the vehicle at the start of the manoeuvre

When manoeuvring, emergency response drivers will:

- Carry out full, all round observations
- Demonstrate safe use of reversing aids
- Be aware of the limitations of reversing aids
- Keep the vehicle's speed under control
- Acurately position the vehicle, without excessive shunting

Emergency response drivers will also demonstrate banksman skills, including:

- Gaining agreement for finishing position
- Normally standing on the left of the vehicle, in view from the driver's nearside mirror
- Keeping the windows down
- Using correct, clear hand and arm signals
- Giving clear verbal directions, such as "Stop"

8. VEHICLE SYMPATHY

"Look after your vehicle and it will look after you".

What is "vehicle sympathy"? - It's adopting a driving style where you do not wear out brakes and pads by harsh, hard or sudden braking. Your use of both the accelerator and the clutch is smooth and there's no clutch riding. You do not allow the engine to labour or over-rev it. Your cornering is smooth and not at an excessive speed thus avoiding wearing the tyres. Who could want to drive any differently?

Components, such as brake pads, tyres, fuel, oil, gearboxes, suspension, steering and clutches can all have dramatically varying longevity, depending on how the vehicle is driven.

There will be occasions that the vehicle needs to be driven hard, but this can still be smooth, providing passenger comfort and at all times, and to "the system". Actions performed by an emergency response driver need to be considerate to the vehicle by minimising unnecessary wear.

Driving a vehicle on emergency response is likely to be very demanding on the vehicle. This is one reason why performing the Vehicle Daily Inspection (VDI) check and defect report is essential. Washing the vehicle at the end of shift will prepare it for the next crew and also ensure a good image of your particular emergency service.

To ensure long term reliability, the vehicle will be subject to a strict servicing programme. Preventive maintenance actions by Fleet Control include vehicle inspection, lubrication, adjustment, cleaning, testing, repair, and/or worn parts replacement.

If your driving style encompasses the advice and guidance given in this manual, then it's likely that you will show consideration to your vehicle and will keep wear to a minimum.

Learning outcomes, with training ...

Response drivers will:

- Carry out a Vehicle Daily Inspection (VDI)
- Report any defects
- Drive the vehicle only if it is roadworthy and safe

Response drivers will demonstrate:

- Vehicle sympathy by driving systematically, such as by selecting the right gear at the correct time in accordance with speed and power requirements.

9. CONTROLLING SKIDS

If your vehicle is skidding on a public road, then you have got it wrong.

Despite modern vehicles being equipped with active safety features such as Anti-Lock Braking (ABS), Traction Control and Electronic Stability Programme (ESP), no electronic system is capable of overcoming the laws of physics. This means that a loss of control, as represented by skidding is still possible.

A skid occurs when the grip between the tyres and the road surface is reduced by certain forces acting upon the vehicle, and one or more wheels start sliding instead of rolling.   This emphasises the need for adequate tyre tread depth and correct tyre pressures.

Most road surfaces provide a satisfactory grip in dry conditions; however, as the speed increases the grip becomes less, especially on smooth surfaces. The weather can influence the grip of the tyres, such as, after a long dry spell, rain will lift oil and rubber deposits making the road very slippery.

Road surfaces where there is an increased risk of skidding include:

- Where there are patches of diesel, for example, where buses or taxis stand.
- On worn sections of road, such as at busy junctions, bends or steep hills.
- Sections of road impregnated with rubber, dust and oil where vehicles regularly pull up sharply.
- Unfavourable cambers on corners and bends.
- Where there is loose gravel on newly surfaced roads.
- Where there are fallen leaves in autumn, the top layer appears dry but the layer underneath may be wet and slippery.
- Ice patches, frost or packed snow on hills, bends and exposed or shaded areas of roads (micro-climates).

Driving to the system should minimise the risk of skids through:

- Good observations of the road

- Speed adjustment where necessary
- Smooth control of steering, braking and gear changing

The risk of skidding can be reduced on poor surfaces, such as snow or ice, by the selection of a higher gear when moving off or travelling at a lower speed.

Below the main types of skid are listed. Understanding the theory is not complete without practical experience. You cannot and must not do this on a public road or any public place. If your training authority no longer provides a skid control course, then it is worth investing in a private one.

Rear Wheel Skid

This is identified by:

- The sound of rear wheels spinning or the vehicle turning broadside.

This type of skid is caused by:

- Fierce acceleration, speed too high, sudden change of direction, excessive or sudden braking.

The remedy is to:

- Remove pressure from the accelerator or brake pedal, depress the clutch pedal and steer in the direction of the skid.

Front Wheel Skid

This is identified by:

- Complete loss of steering; the vehicle continues on original course.

This type of skid is caused by:

- Excessive speed, sudden turn of steering wheel, excessive or sudden braking, or harsh acceleration if a front wheel drive vehicle.

The remedy is to:

- Remove all pressure from accelerator or brake pedal, steer in the direction the vehicle is travelling. Consider selecting a lower gear to reduce speed (this is safer than braking). When the skid is under control, steer gently in the desired direction.

Four Wheel Skid

This is identified by:

- Sensation of an increase in speed, instead of reduction, as vehicle slides forward. There may be a combination of sensations from other types of skids.

This type of skid is caused by:

- Excessive or sudden braking.

The remedy is to:

- Remove pressure from brake pedal and progressively re-apply.

A four wheel skid may be a progression from a front or rear wheel skid, which has not been corrected.

If a skid is experienced, countermeasures should not be excessive or another skid may be induced. When stability has been regained, the vehicle can be driven onto the desired course.

Four causes of skidding:

1. Excessive speed for the existing circumstances
2. Excessive or sudden braking
3. Harsh acceleration
4. Coarse steering in relation to a speed which is not itself excessive

Understeer

Taking a corner too fast, particularly in a front wheel drive vehicle, the front tyres struggle to grip the road and steer the angle requested. As a consequence it will tend to continue straight on. This is understeer, so called because the vehicle is literally turning less than you want it to.

Oversteer

Taking a corner too fast, particularly in a rear wheel drive vehicle, then lifting off the power too sharply in mid-corner will cause a transfer of weight towards the front of the vehicle; the back end will go light and the rear tyres will lose grip. Oversteer is most commonly understood as the rear tyres sliding sideways in a bid to overtake the front tyres.

Most modern vehicles are deliberately engineered to understeer before they oversteer. This is due to understeer being relatively easy and largely intuitive to control and correct. If the worst does happen and control is lost, it's generally safer to crash head-on than sideways.

If you take skid-control training, the instructor may give guidance on emergency braking techniques, dependent on the age of the vehicle. One example is cadence braking technique. This is no longer a requirement because Anti-Lock Brakes (ABS) systems are fitted as standard to modern vehicles. However, should the ABS fail, manual rhythmic pumping of the brakes could help you keep your steering under control.

Learning outcomes, with training ...

Emergency response drivers will be able to state:

- The causes of skids.

Emergency response drivers will recognise:

- The three types of skid.

Emergency response drivers will drive in a style that minimises the risk of skidding, taking into account:

- Tyre condition
- Road surface conditions

In the event of a skid, emergency response drivers will:

- Identify an escape route; for instance, steer towards an open space not a solid object.

Chapter 8

COMMENTARY DRIVING

The Skill of Commentary Driving

The art of good driving begins with concentration.   Commentary driving assists concentration. It helps to think about what we see ahead and how best to respond. It is an effective tool to develop your forward vision and anticipation.

Commentary driving is about being able to put into words what you see, what you are thinking and what you plan to do.

Effective visual scanning is achieved best through training. Speaking out loud while routine driving, will help your driving instructor determine if your prioritisation of hazards is correct.

In modern vehicles, with all the built in comforts of home, it is easy to allow ourselves to become distracted, thinking about something else, when we should be concentrating and planning our driving. It is easy to find ourselves not looking far enough ahead and end up reacting to events rather than anticipating them. This explains why some drivers consider that things happen 'suddenly'. We can overcome this and improve our situational awareness by giving a running commentary of our driving.

The easiest way to get started with a basic commentary is to identify the traffic signs that can be seen, then say how these affect your driving. This can then be developed to identify the physical features of the road, such as a junction or bend, then things that are moving, such as pedestrians and cars, then add to this the condition of the road surface, such as whether it's wet or dry.

From this description of the information seen, you can then add how you are driving to the system, such as positioning correctly; travelling at the right speed; using the best gear and accelerating smoothly with frequent mirror checks.

A running commentary keeps you alert and will improve your observation skills. Your ability to speak out loud, giving the necessary detail, will help to prepare you fully for emergency response driving.

Learning outcomes, with training

An emergency response driver will be able to deliver a descriptive (information) driving commentary in:

- Non-response conditions
- Response conditions

An emergency response driver will be able to deliver a 'system' driving commentary in:

- Non-response conditions
- Response conditions

Deliver an effective driving commentary that:

- Reflects thought process (How you think)
- Reflects visual scanning
- A high visual horizon
- Superior hazard perception skills
- Identifies what action you are going to take

Chapter 9

ROAD TRAFFIC LAW – LEGAL EXEMPTIONS AND NON-EXEMPTIONS

The emergency services are afforded certain privileges in the form of legal exemptions from Road Traffic Law. The claiming of exemptions has to be justified and is dependent on particular road, traffic and weather conditions.

The over-riding responsibility for safety rests with the emergency service driver. Because of the urgency, response drivers will, where possible, attempt to make good progress through traffic. This involves claiming established exemptions where it would otherwise hinder the purpose for which the response vehicle is being used on that occasion.

There is no automatic "right" to claim an exemption. Where they are not justified, the response driver's judgement can be called to account by the service, and in the event of a serious collision, a court of law.

1. **Exceeding a speed limit.**

   The statutory speed limit can be exceeded, but only if safe to do so.

2. **Contravening a red light traffic signal, including at pedestrian crossings.**

   A red traffic light signal can be treated as a "give way".

3. **Contravening a keep left/right sign.**

   Emergency drivers may pass on the opposite side of keep left/right signs where there is no other alternative

The full range of exemptions is listed below. They are presented using a mnemonic – "**MOS UP PETS PEE**" to assist learning requirements, particularly for the ambulance industry.

Front line Driver – Emergency Response Exemptions

Motorway regulations

Observing keep left/right signs

Parking within the zig-zag area of a pedestrian crossing

Stopping on a clearway

Using audible warnings at night

Parking within areas controlled by double white/yellow/red lines

Parking on the offside of the road at night

Exceeding statutory speed limits

Treating a red traffic light as a give way

Stopping the engine whilst parked

Parking on footway, verge or central reservation

Entering a bus lane or street

Entering a pedestrian precinct

Four additional exemptions have been included in the above list

1. Parking or driving on a cycle track

2. Parking at a designated bus stop

3. Parking across a dropped kerb and double parking

4. Stopping within a yellow box junction

Front line Driver – Main non-exemptions

These non-exemptions apply when driving on response and non-response journeys:

1. Dangerous driving.

A person who drives a mechanically propelled vehicle dangerously on a road or other public place is guilty of an offence. A person is to be regarded as driving dangerously if the way he or she drives falls far below what would be expected of a competent and careful driver, and it would be obvious to a competent and careful driver that driving in that way would be dangerous. Examples include driving the wrong way along a dual carriageway; driving on a footpath towards pedestrians; failing to stop for police with an element of excess speed; crashing a vehicle into another with intent of doing so and failing to stop thereafter.

2. **Careless driving (Driving without due care and attention).**

   A person who drives a mechanically propelled vehicle on a road or other public place without due care and attention is guilty of an offence. A person is to be regarded as driving without due care and attention if (and only if) the way he or she drives falls below what would be expected of a competent and careful driver. Examples include tailgating and undertaking; failing to stop at a stop and give way sign; contravening several red traffic lights in sequence.

3. **Driving without reasonable consideration**

   A person is to be regarded as driving without reasonable consideration for other persons only if those persons are inconvenienced by his or her driving. Examples include remaining in an overtaking lane; failing to give way to priority traffic at a junction, failing to give way to the right at a roundabout and splashing a pedestrian with water from the road surface.

Other examples can be found on the Crown Prosecution Service (CPS) website:

www.cps.gov.uk/driving-offences

Each offence is looked at individually. Ultimately, it comes down to varying burdens of proof; with "Dangerous driving" (the standard of driving must fall "far below" that of a careful and competent driver) being the highest with "Inconsiderate driving" (where someone is only inconvenienced) being the lowest.

It is possible for a case of "Dangerous Driving" to be downgraded to a matter of "Careless Driving" so it can be heard summarily at a Magistrates Court rather than a Crown Court.

Other non-exemptions include:

• Crossing or straddling a solid white line nearest to you down the middle of the road (other than those listed in the Highway Code or if you pass a maintenance vehicle, a pedal cyclist or a horse being ridden all of which must be travelling at 10mph or less)

- Dangerous Parking

- Driving without wearing a seat belt, other than when stated in the Highway Code

- Failing to stop if involved in a road traffic collision

- Failing to obey traffic lights controlling a railway level crossing or fire station

- Failing to obey a "one way traffic" sign*

- Failing to obey a "no entry" sign*

- Failing to obey any other "prohibitive sign", such as "no right turn" or "no U turn"*

- Failing to obey a "stop" or "give way" sign*

- Using a mobile phone (or similar device) whilst driving or in control of a vehicle

* Unless instructed to do so by a uniformed police officer, Highways Agency Traffic Officer (HATO) or traffic warden.

Patient Transport Services (PTS) Ambulance – Exemptions

The drivers of Patient Transport Service (PTS) ambulances have entitlement to the listed exemptions below.

- Stopping the engine whilst parked

- Stopping on a clearway

- Parking within the zig-zag lines of a pedestrian crossing

- Parking in areas controlled by double white/yellow lines

- Parking on the offside of the road at night

- Parking on footway/verge/central reservation

- Parking across a dropped kerb

- Parking at a designated bus stop

- Parking on a cycle track

- Double parking

And as you would expect, there are PTS non-exemptions.

PTS Ambulance Driver - Non-exemptions

- Dangerous Driving
- Careless Driving
- Dangerous Parking
- Driving without a seat belt, other than when stated in the Highway Code

Road Traffic Law

In addition to knowing the exemptions from normal traffic regulations, emergency response drivers must maintain a sound knowledge of Road Traffic Law as well as any Service policies and procedures.

All relevant aspects of motoring law are published in the Highway Code. These include all rules that state "must" or "must not". If you disobey these, then you are committing a criminal offence. A failure to comply with advisory rules such as "should" or "should not" or "do" and "do not" may be used as evidence in Court to establish liability.

Also, under civil law, there is case precedent that requires drivers to maintain the expected standard, and to drive in a manner that conforms to the standard for protecting others. McCrone v Riding 1938.

Guidelines on sentencing issued by the Court of Appeal state "drivers must know that, if a person is killed as a result of their driving dangerously a custodial sentence will normally be imposed no matter what the mitigating circumstances."

Students on the blue-light ambulance course must complete a workbook that searches for information about Roadcraft and response/non-response driving. Ambulance students' knowledge is checked with a "law exam" that currently consists of 37 questions. The pass mark is 100%. Success particularly depends on knowing all the exemptions and non-exemptions to road traffic law. There are other questions regarding speed limits for types of vehicle; traffic light signals and road markings; vehicle lighting regulations and applying motorway exemptions. You will also need to be able to briefly explain/define the term "red mist".

Useful additional advice ...

Seat belts: From both a legal, and a health and safety perspective, all members of the ambulance crew and patients must wear a seat belt. However, in the circumstances where the attendant needs to be stood up to provide genuine medical emergency treatment to a patient, then seat belt use is not a requirement. Particularly when driving on emergency response, the driver must be aware that the attendant is not seated so that verbal warnings of potential vehicle movements can be given before impending road hazards such as speed humps.

When the ambulance is moving, any patient who is being transported on a stretcher trolley in the treatment area must be safely strapped in.

Parking exemptions: When parking at any incident, think about access for the patient and crew and also whether there is a safer alternative. At a Road Traffic Collision consider maximum protection to other road users and follow service policy on "Fend-Off" / "Fend-In" and "In-Line" parking.

Stopping the engine whilst parked: Operate engine "runlock". This function allows the driver to leave the vehicle with engine running with the ignition keys removed and the vehicle locked. The engine will therefore be able to continue charging the batteries that provide power for the vehicles equipment, including the Mobile Data Terminal (MDT).

Entering a bus lane: Only use with-flow bus lanes, unless it provides the only access. There is a risk of being blocked when using a contra-flow bus lane.

Collisions: It should be stressed that if you have a collision, not matter how minor it might seem; such as an impact with another vehicles door mirror, you

MUST STOP and give your own and vehicle owners name and address and registration number to anyone having reasonable grounds for requiring them.

Personal Protective Equipment (PPE): For maximum visual warning, wear your hi-viz jacket, for instance when performing banksman duties. On the public road, particularly a motorway, the front of your jacket needs to be zipped up closed.

Human factors that affect emergency response driving

The TSO book,"Roadcraft" gives a list of human factors that can put the emergency response driver at risk of a collision. These can also be associated with confrontational behaviour with third parties or even crew members. The list includes distraction due to multi-tasking; driving stress; operational stressors; time pressure and the purpose of the journey; "noble cause" risk taking and "red mist".

As response drivers, we have a responsibility for ourselves. We need to be at our best, maintaining a consistently calm and professional approach to our driving. This may not be so easy in very demanding and challenging working conditions.

Staying alert and avoiding tiredness isn't always easy because of irregular shift patterns. There are some simple practical steps that can be taken, such as checking our seat position; vehicle ventilation; taking regular rest breaks; drinking coffee and taking short brisk walks.

Physiological factors can affect your concentration and reaction times. These can be caused by minor illnesses, such as a cold or hay fever; medication; residual blood alcohol; low blood sugar (arising from hunger) and life stress (such as bereavement).

Operational stressors can cause negative emotional feelings in demanding situations. Examples of these given in "Roadcraft" include impatience; intolerance; impulsiveness; anger; frustration and personalisation.

How we manage and control these factors begins with recognising the symptoms described. First re-read and reflect on the advice given in this book in Chapter 1 on Driver Responsibility. Then check through Chapter 10 and Appendix 1. These cover the technical information needed for Driving on Blues and Twos, including the JPLAN, along with the formal requirements of Section 19 of the Road Safety Act (2006). Where necessary, have a professional discussion with your trainer or Course Director about the issues flagged here and any personal concerns that you might have.

Learning outcomes, with training ...

Emergency response drivers must be able to state:

- What is meant by the term 'exemption'
- The exemptions from traffic regulations permissible on a blue-light call
- With examples, when and how these exemptions can be used
- How 'standard of care'; 'duty of care' and 'negligence' are defined in civil law
- The reasons for complying with driving legislation and regulations and the consequences of disregarding these.

Emergency response drivers must be able to demonstrate in practice a high standard of safe driving skills for:

- Routine driving, in compliance with the current Road Traffic Law and the Highway Code
- Blue-light calls, being able to justify the use of any the exemptions claimed

Emergency response drivers must be able to:

- Demonstrate ability to predict and safely respond to the behavioural changes of other drivers
- Manage confrontational behaviour when responding to emergencies.

Emergency response drivers must be able to identify situations where conflict involves:

- Vehicle crew members
- Others, including all other road users

Emergency response drivers must be able to:

- State the techniques to combat the effects of stress when responding to emergencies
- Reflect on own driving practice in emergency response situations.

Emergency response drivers must be able to state the:

- procedure should a response vehicle be involved in a collision
- service guidelines on legal matters involving collisions.

Emergency response drivers must also be able to:

- state the elements of the high speed driver training regulations
- drive in compliance with high speed driver training regulations

Emergency response drivers must also be able to state the situations when to use the following vehicle positions:

- In line
- Fend in
- Fend off

Chapter 10

DRIVING ON BLUES AND TWOS
(USE OF VISUAL AND AUDIBLE WARNINGS)

Intelligent use of blue flashing lights and two tone sirens provide an early warning of an approaching vehicle engaged in an emergency journey. They help to elicit swift, safe progress by gaining the attention of other road users. Displaying visual and audible warnings does not necessarily guarantee any creation of space or passage through.

- **Blue flashing lights.** As a routine, the blue flashing lights need to remain on while en-route to the scene of an emergency. They are necessary while claiming exemptions from road traffic law, such as exceeding speed limits, proceeding through red traffic signals and passing keep left/right signs on the wrong side.

Unless protecting the scene of an emergency, such as a road traffic collision, the blue flashing lights should normally be switched off. Be guided by police officers in attendance, especially if the call is on a motorway.

- **Audible warnings.** When switching the siren on, the first sound is usually the "wail". This sound pattern carries the furthest distance and is used when making normal progress. The other siren is the "yelp". This sound pattern carries less distance and is suited to a closed or busy traffic environment. For instance, at road junctions, blind bends or other such hazards. Other sirens may be available such as the "French horn" and "Phaser". Using some discretion, alternating the various sirens will emphasise your presence. In busy or complex traffic conditions this can help create a passage through.

The direction of audible sirens may not be obvious to drivers. Motorists need plenty of time to react, and are prone to panic or make irrational manoeuvres. Do switch the sirens off when near horses, including those in horse boxes. Also switch them off when close to other animals and when stationary. Where possible, we also switch the sirens off when passing a funeral cortege. Ambulance service drivers should turn the sirens off when close to a hospital destination.

Responding to an emergency call? Check the "JPLAN".

The "JPLAN" helps response drivers make intelligent use of the blue lights and sirens.

Justification. Justifying claims to exemptions while on an emergency call, depends on the road and traffic conditions encountered at the time

Proportionate. Response to the emergency call should be measured and proportionate, taking personal steps to avoid the experience of "red mist"

Least intrusive. Good assessment and planning of how to use the blue lights and sirens. Use the "seven second rule". This will create a positive impact on the traffic situation ahead

Accountability. The emergency response has to be auditable. That is, be attached to a genuine 999 emergency call or accredited driver training where a Computer Aided Dispatch (CAD) number has requested and agreed (possibly with conditions) by the regional police control

Necessity. It might not always be necessary to use the emergency response equipment. There are some occasions when you need to turn off the sirens and possibly also the blue lights, for instance at a red signal crossing a fast road.

Correctly responding to an emergency call is **NOT** about driving at high speed, it's about **safe progression** through traffic.

Applying the system of vehicle control.

The system of vehicle control should be applied to all driving, including emergency response:

- Information - Identify road and traffic features ahead

- Position – on a two way road, quite often "extended" to partially or wholly cross the centre of the road to face oncoming traffic

- Speed – reduced for both open and closed junctions and varied to suit traffic signals. Walking pace, particularly at a closed junction, and very little faster where the junction is open. If the crossing traffic is fast, comply with the red stop signal and turn off the blues and twos

- Gear – with a manual box, block change down, appropriate to the speed
- Gear – with an automatic box, lock down to lower appropriate gear when travelling downhill and on bends
- Acceleration – smoothly to suit prevailing traffic and road conditions.

When approaching traffic congestion

- Look for the "line of least resistance"
- Position the vehicle relative to that line
- Where progress can be made, use "wail" siren; be prepared to change to the "yelp" to suit your driving plan
- Where no progress is possible, switch off audible sirens and wait
- When passing a line of stationary or slow vehicles, our speed must be reduced sufficiently to take into account any "unexpected actions by other road users"
- To get the maximum attention, the "yelp" siren works really well at junctions in towns because the sound bounces around quite a lot. The "wail" siren is better for warning traffic in the further distance.

At road works

Proceed only if the exit can been seen and it is safe to do so. If the exit cannot be seen, unless directed by a responsible person, wait for the green light.

Primary Route Dual carriageways

When joining or crossing against a red light, switch the blues and twos off until it is clear to proceed. This minimises the risk of third party rear end shunts, which will delay your response to the emergency call.

Overtaking at solid white lines in the centre of the road

We do not have any exemption that allows us to cross solid white lines to overtake. Motorists in the main are unaware that they are expected to STOP before we can legally cross these lines to overtake. For this reason we maintain "silent running", that is, without audible warnings, extending the separation distance with the vehicle immediately ahead. This minimises pressure on the driver in front; reducing the risk of this driver pulling over into a position where it will be difficult for us to get passed, such as on a blind bend.

Response vehicle – emergency lights and siren buttons

These vary from vehicle to vehicle. Before driving the vehicle, as part of the VDI, this equipment should be checked. Be considerate of others and maintain Service Policy on location for checking sirens.

Verbal intervention

Particularly while engaged on an emergency response call, where a patient is being transported to a hospital, the driver should inform the attendant verbally when approaching hazards which may affect vehicle movements. For example, shout "SPEED HUMPS", "UNEVEN ROAD" or "CATTLE GRID". This will help the attendant ensure that they are safely restrained or suitably positioned.

Advice given to the public in the Highway Code:

Emergency vehicles. You should look and listen for ambulances, fire engines, police or other emergency vehicles using flashing blue, red or green lights, headlights or sirens. When one approaches do not panic. Consider the route of the emergency vehicle and take appropriate action to let it pass. If necessary, pull to the side of the road and stop, but do not endanger other road users.

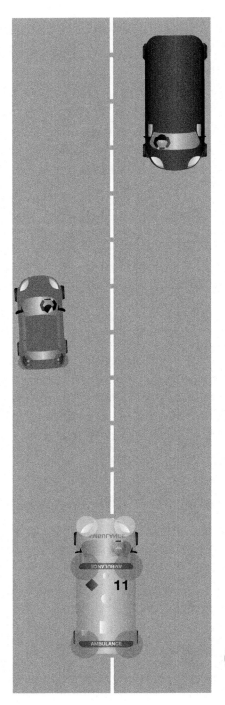

Closing Gap between Target and Approaching Driver –
"Moment of Realisation"

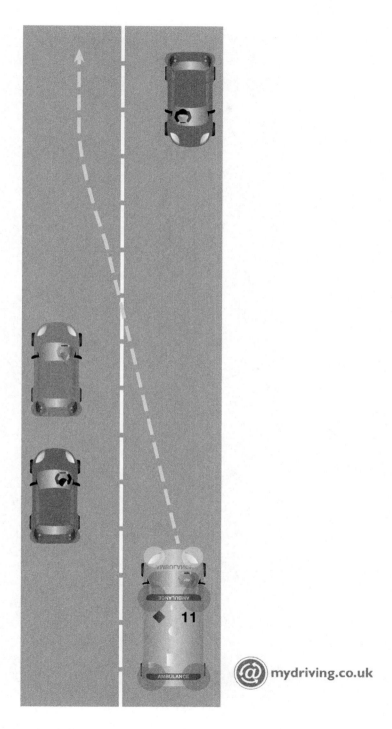

Position of Dominance – "Extended Road Position"

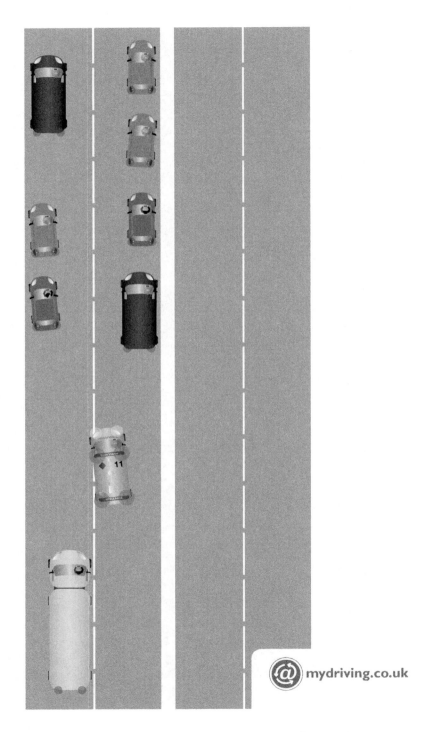

Very Slow or Stationary Traffic – The "Parting of the Waves"

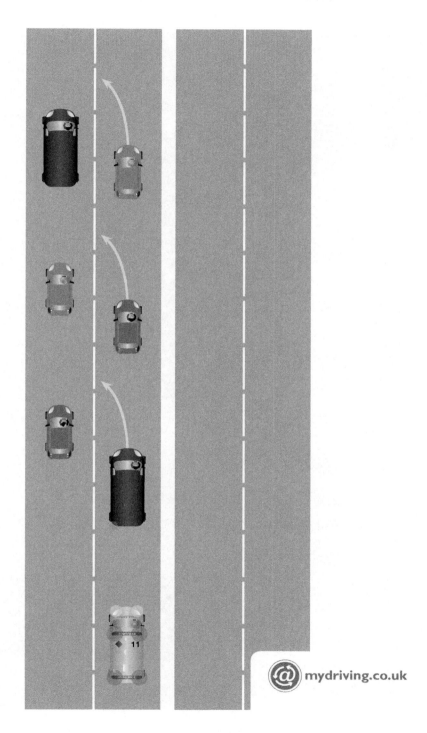

mydriving.co.uk

Moving Traffic – "Extended Road Positioning"

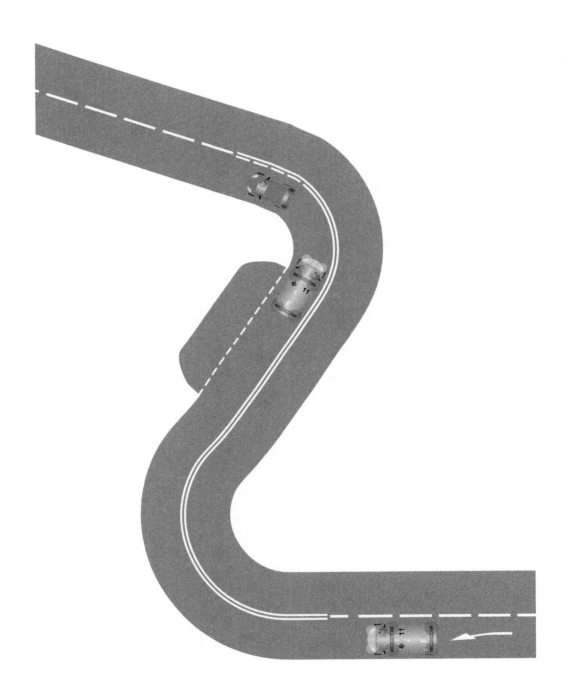

Double Solid White Lines – No Exemption to Cross

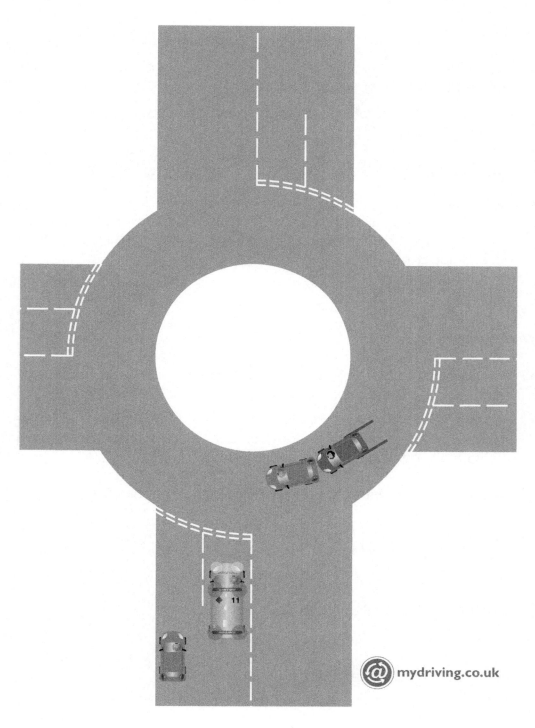

Third party late response to approaching ambulance
Drivers need enough time to respond to emergency lights and sirens

We would add;

- We do NOT expect you to risk damage to your tyres, wheels or steering by bumping up kerbs to make way for us
- We do not expect you to put yourself in danger by crossing red traffic lights to make way for us
- We do not expect you to risk road camera fines by, for example, moving in to bus lanes during hours of operation to make way for us
- We would however, appreciate your co-operation by looking well ahead and choosing sensible places to pull over. If possible avoid stopping before bends, brows of hills or narrow sections of roads where we may have difficulty passing.
- The Highway Code provides advice to drivers when seeing an emergency vehicle.

We would further add;

- Don't overtake a blue light vehicle on a motorway or dual carriageway... or you might find yourself caught in the incident it's heading for
- Sirens and flashing blue lights could belong to more than one emergency vehicle - so keep your eyes and ears open. A second emergency vehicle will normally be using a different siren sound.

An excellent video is available from the Guild of Experienced Motorists (GEM), available online at:

- www.bluelightaware.org.uk

Learning outcomes, with training ...

Emergency response drivers will know how to operate the:

- Visual warnings, partially and fully
- Audible warnings by changing tones and switch them off

Emergency response drivers will be able to state how:

- Audible and visual warnings can assist with safe progress to an emergency call.

Emergency response drivers will be able to demonstrate appropriate judgement calls for using the:

- Wail siren tone
- Yelp siren tone
- Other tones fitted, such as phaser and French horn.

Emergency response drivers will be able to state:

- The isolated occasions where a discretion may be used to drive on blue lights without using any tones
- The implications arising from any collision where the tones are not in use.

Appendix 1

Section 19 of the Road Safety Act (2006)

Section 19 of the Road Safety Act (2006) is expected to replace Section 87 of the Road Traffic Regulation Act (1984) in relation to exemptions from speed limits for certain vehicle purposes.

There is currently no legal requirement for a driver to be trained at driving safely at high speeds when using a vehicle for a purpose that is exempt from speed limits.

Implementation of the new section will make it an offence to exceed speed limits for fire, ambulance, police or Serious Organised Crime Agency (SOCA) purposes unless a vehicle's driver "has satisfactorily completed a course of training in the driving of vehicles at high speed".

Organisations providing emergency response already provide training to meet their duty of care for staff and the public, as well as Health & Safety responsibilities. The proposed standard is intended as a minimum and not expected to make up the entire competency for driving on blues and twos.

The proposed driving standard of the **High Speed Driver Training** (HSDT) Course is set out within a single Unit. This is made up of five elements containing the competences that a driver must display at speeds above the speed limit. Each element states that the following 'attitudes and behaviours' must be demonstrated at all times when driving:

- Give priority to public safety
- Demonstrate a calm, considerate and professional manner
- Control the tendency to "personalise"
- Recognise and respond appropriately to the effects of fatigue, adrenaline, stress and other physical and physiological factors that may impair judgment, performance and decision making
- Concentrate on driving in the face of any other distractions.

Speed choice is a competency associated with the greatest risk of collision. As with the other exemptions, a justification has to be made. The driver has discretion as to when and where to exceed the speed limit on a road or for a vehicle, wisely and as safely as is possible given need and circumstances.

The High Speed Driver Training Code of Practice (CoP) published by the Department for Transport (DfT) indicates that "high speed should be construed as any speed which exceeds that of any statutory speed limit in force on the road at that time. It might also be interpreted as a speed which is below the statutory speed limit but in excess of a speed which would be appropriate to the prevailing road conditions at the time."

- Individual Service policies will continue to provide guidelines as to this and the maximum margins recommended for exceeding posted and National Speed Limits.

The right attitudes and behaviours have relevance in this respect, making it incumbent on the driver to control any feelings of "red mist". Use of speed must always be appropriate. That is, you can stop in the distance you can see to be clear.

The high speed competencies detailed in each of the five elements listed here are a minimum standard, intended for inclusion within a bespoke driver training course provided by each emergency service.

Element 1 Demonstrate basic driving skills

The focus of this element is to ensure the driver possesses the essential knowledge, understanding and skills required to drive vehicles competently, beginning with:

- Complete basic vehicle safety checks, identifying, reporting and documenting obvious defects
- Familiarising with the vehicle's controls before driving

On a typical variety of road and traffic conditions within statutory speed limits:

- Recognise, assess and manage hazards through effective observation, anticipation and planning
- Steer the vehicle accurately to maintain a safe and appropriate course
- Control the vehicle safely and accurately through the use of accelerator, brakes, gears and clutch as appropriate to the circumstances
- Make progress appropriate to the conditions and circumstances
- Approach and negotiate corners safely
- Position the vehicle safely as appropriate to the circumstances
- Use appropriate signals and respond correctly to the signals of other road users
- Select safe and appropriate locations to park and manoeuvre the vehicle
- Call on the assistance of others before completing difficult manoeuvres
- Reverse, manoeuvre and park the vehicle safely.

You need to know and understand the following:

- Organisational policy and directives covering driving
- Relevant health and safety legislation
- Human aspects of emergency service driving
- The Highway Code / Road Traffic legislation
- Manufacturer's instructions

This element provides the foundation for the other four elements. It will therefore be necessary to complete this element first, before progressing to the other High Speed Driving Training elements.

Element 2   Prepare and drive vehicles at high speed

The focus of this element is on vehicle preparation, the system of vehicle control, driver attitude and health and safety. This element covers:

Use of speed

- In excess of the statutory speed limit for the road / vehicle
- Within statutory speed limit but in excess of traffic flow

Locations

- Major / minor roads
- Urban / rural settings

Traffic volume

- Low / high

Road surfaces / Visibility

- Good / poor

You must be able to prepare the vehicle, first ensuring that you are authorised to drive the vehicle. Prepare and familiarise yourself with the vehicle and its controls. You need to be able to carry out required checks to:

- Tyres
- Brakes
- Fluid levels
- Lights
- Sound equipment
- Safety equipment
- Bodywork / cleanliness of the vehicle
- Operational equipment

You will also need to:

- Eensure the vehicle is fit for purpose during and after use
- Identify, report and record any defects or damage prior to and following use and take the correct action in regard to these
- Ensure that any equipment required to be with the vehicle is present and in working order
- Keep accurate and complete documentation as required relating to your use of the vehicle.

Formulating and implementing driving plans

You will need to demonstrate ability to:

- Gather information at an early stage through accurate observations and the use of other senses
- Use this information to correctly anticipate all driving situations
- Use observation links effectively
- Use information and anticipation to formulate flexible driving plans
- Implement driving plans to safely negotiate all driving situations.

You must be able to do the following:

- Make progress whilst showing restraint

  This involves accurately judging the speed of your own and other vehicles relative to your proposed actions and the circumstances, taking account of distance / make progress whilst maintaining the need for restraint and safety.

- Control the vehicle

  This involves safe and smooth use of the accelerator; applying the required amount of braking at the correct time. When driving manual vehicles, select the correct gear for the circumstances by smooth and accurate use of gears and clutch. Steer the vehicle accurately, adapting steering techniques as necessary when manoeuvring.

- Positioning

  This involves positioning the vehicle correctly when following and overtaking other vehicles / when negotiating corners and bends. Position the vehicle to obtain the best view with regard to safety. Adopt the safest road position at all times in relation to existing road and traffic positions.

- Cornering

  This involves assessing corners and bends correctly and accurately. Negotiating corners and bends, taking account of all relevant factors.

- Making and interpreting signals

  This involves making appropriate signals to other road users using indicators; lights; audible signals and hand signals. Correctly interpret and act on signals from other road users.

You must be able to do the following:

- Overtaking

  Identify, plan and execute all overtaking manoeuvres safely when passing stationary objects and moving vehicles. Apply the correct degree of restraint at all times.

You need to know and understand the following:

- Organisational policy and directives covering driving
- Relevant health and safety legislation, including dynamic risk assessment
- Human Aspects of Emergency Response Driving
- The Highway Code / Road Traffic legislation
- Relevant sections of Roadcraft – Police Drivers' Handbook
- Manufacturers' instructions.

Training for Elements 1 and 2 can run simultaneously.

Element 3   Drive vehicles at high-speed motorways and multi-lane carriageways

The focus of this element is on driving vehicles safely at speed on motorways and multi-lane carriageways. This element covers the following:

Use of speed

- In excess of the statutory speed limit for the road / vehicle
- Within statutory speed limit but in excess of traffic flow

Traffic volume

- Low / high

Weather conditions / Road surfaces and visibility

- Good / poor

Locations

- Motorways / multi-carriageways
- urban / rural settings

You must be able to do the following:

- Follow the correct procedure for joining the motorway/multi-carriageway road
- Adopt the correct lane for existing road and traffic conditions
- Adjust speed appropriately for type of road and traffic conditions
- Follow the correct procedure for exiting the motorway/multi-carriageway road.

You need to know and understand the following:

- Relevant sections of the Highway Code, including the meaning of all road signs, matrix signals, marker boards and cats eyes
- Relevant sections of Roadcraft – Police Drivers' Handbook
- The correct procedures for stopping on, and setting off from, the roadside or hard shoulder.

Element 4   Undertake an emergency response using a vehicle

The focus of this element is on undertaking an emergency response using an emergency vehicle. This element covers the following:

Use of speed

- in excess of the statutory speed limit for the road / vehicle
- within statutory speed limit but in excess of traffic flow

Locations

- Motorways / multi-carriageways
- Major / minor roads
- Urban / rural settings

Road surfaces / Visibility / Weather Conditions

- Good / poor

Traffic volume

- Low / high

Time of Day

- Daylight / darkness

You must be able to do the following:

- Ensure that an emergency response is justifiable and should be maintained
- Ensure that there is justification for taking advantage of your speed exemptions
- Make effective use of emergency warning equipment, when appropriate
- Anticipate and respond to the actions of other road users

- Make safe and appropriate progress
- Maintain a duty of care whilst using speed limit exemption
- Ensure all actions are consistent with legal requirements and organisational policies

You need to know and understand the following:

- Organisational policy and directives concerning emergency response
- Relevant health and safety and Human Rights legislation
- The Highway Code / Road Traffic legislation
- Relevant sections of Roadcraft – Police Drivers' Handbook
- Communication and audible and visual warning procedures

Element 5   Avoid and correct skids when driving an emergency vehicle

The focus of this element is on driving in a way that minimises the risk of skidding and being able to correct a skid when it occurs. This Element covers the following:

Types of skid

- Front wheel
- Rear wheel
- Four wheel

Vehicles

- Without active safety devices
- With active safety devices

You must be able to do the following:

- Identify the causation and types of skid
- Drive the vehicle in a manner that minimises the risk of skidding
- Apply appropriate corrective action to the type of vehicle being driven.

No exemption from prosecution

In the case of both current and updated exemptions from speed limits, there is, and will be no tolerance of a driver using a vehicle in an irresponsible manner. A driver can still be prosecuted for careless or dangerous driving if their behaviour warrants such action.

Appendix 2

Emergency Response Driving Instructors

An increasing number of Driver Vehicle Standards Agency (DVSA) Approved Driving Instructors (ADI) provide training to the emergency services, including the blue-light response element.

Driving Instructors delivering this training, are typically drawn from the ranks of each Emergency Service. External driving instructors who work freelance often are found to be former Class One (or equivalent) police drivers or instructors.

Any ADI (car) considering a career move into this industry will need to have a very strong driving background. The best way for an instructor to develop their own driving ability, is to take further driving courses that are associated with the police driving standards published in "Roadcraft".

A first step for ADIs has to be taking the DVSA's "Fleet Register" qualification. This provides a good introduction to the driving techniques advocated in "Roadcraft". Accredited fleet trainer courses will also provide practical exercises in coaching techniques. Details of how to become a Fleet Driver Trainer can be found at:

- www.gov.uk/become-a-fleet-driver-trainer/overview

You can make a postcode search for an accredited fleet driver training course at:

- www.gov.uk/fleet-driver-training-courses

ADIs can also get help improving and developing their driving skills from the:

- Institute of Advanced Motorists (IAM) and/or
- Royal Society for the Prevention of Accidents (RoSPA)
- High Performance Course (HPC)

Both the IAM and RoSPA are charities that run civilian Advanced Driving Tests. The IAM provide a "Masters" advanced driving award that embraces the 4 levels of the GDE (Goals for Driver Education) matrix. Driving commentary is mandatory to achieve this qualification. RoSPA offer an excellent Diploma in

Driving Instruction for candidates who achieve the "Gold" Standard on their advanced test.

Beyond IAM and RoSPA, you can consider taking training on the High Performance Course (HPC). This is the original specialist advanced driving course, establish in the 1960s, that has been developed to meet modern driving needs. A web search will quickly provide you with more information and details.

Having achieved a very high standard of driving, networking within the industry can help you achieve your goal. To this end, consider becoming a member of the:

- Association of Industrial Road Safety Officers (AIRSO)

AIRSO hold excellent meetings and specialist conferences that you will benefit from. Again, run a web search for more information.

From time to time, police driving schools recruit civilian driving instructors from the ranks of the ADI industry. As a member of the IAM and/or RoSPA, you can look out for the advertisements for vacancies that appear in their subscriber's magazines.

If you prefer a career in the ambulance service, depending on the Trust or private service, or if you passed your car test after 1 January 1997, you will need to take and pass the driving test for Category C1 Heavy Goods Vehicle. This is because some emergency ambulance vehicles are in this category. Before you can take training on how to give instruction and coaching, you will need to hold this license for a minimum of three years.

Similarly, to become a fire appliance driving instructor, you will need to pass the Category C driving test and then hold this license for a minimum of three years.

Emergency response vehicles do not have dual controls. Instructors in these vehicles need to have a skill-set to meet the needs of the work. Well-developed and excellent communication skills should be demonstrated:

- By an ability to make quick decisions and give clear positive instruction
- With confidence and calm
- By a firm but tactful approach to students

Having good observation and situational judgement in traffic conditions is not enough. Whether by giving direct instruction or using coaching techniques; guidance has to be communicated effectively to new response drivers in a way that suits them.

This work is probably NOT for the average ADI, without significant professional training, mentoring and considerable personal development.

Continuing Professional Development (CPD) for Emergency Response Instructors

CPD is a process of tracking and documenting the skills, knowledge and experience that you gain both formally and informally as you work, beyond any initial training. It's a record of what you experience, learn and then apply in the workplace.

Within the ambulance industry, all driving instructors are formally required to keep a record of their Continuing Professional Development. A time frame is in place where all instructors will gain the following awards:

- Level 4 Certificate in Education and Training – this replaces the Certificate in Teaching in the Lifelong Learning Sector (CTLLS)
- Certificate in Assessing Vocational Achievement (CAVA)
- Level 4 Diploma in Emergency Response Ambulance Driving Instruction (Conversion award for qualified instructors)
- Approved Driving Instructor (ADI)

Appendix 3

Ambulance Driver Training

It's more than thirty years since 999 ambulances provided a simple "scoop and scoot" service to hospital. Modern ambulance crews provide life-saving pre-hospital emergency care and treatment. To become an ambulance driver, you need to be, or taking training to become a Paramedic, an Emergency Care Assistant or an Ambulance Care Assistant.

- There are two principal ways to train as a paramedic:

    1. An approved full-time university course
    2. Working as a student paramedic with an ambulance trust.

- Emergency Care Assistants (ECAs) work for NHS Trusts or private ambulance services. They respond to emergency calls, along with a qualified practitioner, such as a paramedic and carry out emergency care at the scene.

    The initial clinical training for new ECAs, usually takes around six to nine weeks. As well as routine and emergency response driving, this covers:

    1. Moving and handling techniques
    2. Emergency first aid
    3. Basic patient skills.

- NHS Trusts no longer train entrants for the role of Ambulance Technician - Emergency Medical Technician (EMT).

You can find help on how to become a paramedic or an ECA here:

www.how2become.com/courses/paramedic

All clinical training includes frequent practical assessments and written exams. Before working unsupervised, students can expect to work under the guidance of a trained supervisor.

- Ambulance Care Assistants and Patient Transport Service (PTS) drivers usually have an initial two to three week training course. The role involves lifting and helping patients in and out of the ambulance. They make sure patients are safe and comfortable during the journey and arrive on time for their appointment. The PTS role does not include emergency driving response duties.

Emergency response ambulance drivers must be able to navigate busy streets safely, without endangering the public or the patient being transported. To achieve this, a new qualifying standard has been devised. This is of benefit not only to ambulance drivers, but also their instructors, making it very clear what the driving requirements are, for both routine and non-response driving.

Ambulance Driving – The Qualifying Standard

Since 2016, the Qualifying Standard presented here has set the benchmark for ambulance driver training. The necessary learning outcomes are divided into two units:

1. Be able to prepare, drive and manoeuvre ambulance vehicles (Level 2)
2. Be able to drive an ambulance vehicle in emergency and non-emergency situations (Level 3)

Unit 1: Prepare, Drive and Manoeuvre Ambulance Vehicles

Unit Summary

This unit assesses the knowledge, skills and understanding required to prepare, drive and manoeuvre ambulance vehicles, including pre-driving checks, navigation, the effects of adverse conditions and managing confrontational behaviour.

Learning Outcome – The learner will:	Assessment Criteria – The learner can:
1. Be able to carry out a pre-shift vehicle daily inspection and pre driving checks.	1.1 State the legal requirements when checking a vehicle for: • Compliance • Safety
	1.2 State reasons and legal requirements for performing a pre driving check.
	1.3 Outline the order of a pre driving check.
	1.4 Summarise the capabilities and limitations of a range of vehicles.
	1.5 Carry out a daily inspection on a range of vehicles.
	1.6 Carry out a pre driving check on a range of vehicles.
	1.7 Complete the correct documentation when carrying out the vehicle checks.
	1.8 Outline actions to take if vehicle defects are identified.

Learning Outcome – The learner will:	Assessment Criteria – The learner can:
2. Be able to comply with current legislation and driving regulations at all times.	2.1 Explain reasons for complying with legislation and driving regulations.
	2.2 Outline the consequences of disregarding legislation and driving regulations.
	2.3 Explain exemptions available for routine ambulance driving.
	2.4 Explain actions required for incident management when: • Incident involves service vehicle • Coming across an incident
	2.5 Comply with the Highway Code at all times when in control of a vehicle.

Learning Outcome – The learner will:	Assessment Criteria – The learner can:
3. Be able to use vehicles' braking systems.	3.1 State considerations for using brakes.
	3.2 Explain why a static and mobile brake test is carried out.
	3.3 Explain how a static and mobile brake test is carried out.
	3.4 Explain how braking can provide a ride that meets individual patients' needs.
	3.5 Describe what is meant by tapered braking.
	3.6 Use tapered braking.
	3.7 Use a vehicle's braking system effectively when driving.

Learning Outcome – The learner will:	Assessment Criteria – The learner can:
4. Be able to use vehicles' steering systems	4.1 Explain factors that affect steering.
	4.2 State rules for vehicle steering.
	4.3 State considerations when cornering to include: • Approach • Positioning • Forces acting on vehicle
	4.4 Explain effects on cornering speeds of: • Vehicle condition • Type
	4.5 Identify limit point when cornering.
	4.6 Steer a vehicle according to the rules of steering.
	4.7 Negotiate a corner when driving.

Learning Outcome – The learner will:	Assessment Criteria – The learner can:
5. Be able to use vehicles' transmission systems during routine driving.	5.1 Explain the use of gears in relation to economical driving.
	5.2 Select appropriate gear to drive economically.
	5.3 Use vehicle's transmission system effectively during routine driving.

Learning Outcome – The learner will:	Assessment Criteria – The learner can:
6. Be able to vary the speed of the vehicle.	6.1 State the advantages of using acceleration sense.
	6.2 Explain when acceleration sense should be applied.
	6.3 Use the accelerator to vary vehicle speed.
	6.4 Use engine braking to vary vehicle speed in a range of conditions.

Learning Outcome – The learner will:	Assessment Criteria – The learner can:
7. Be able to use procedures for multi-lane carriageways and motorway driving.	7.1 Explain procedures for multi-lane carriageway and motorway driving when: • Joining • Exiting • Changing lane • Lane discipline
	7.2 Describe types and meaning of road signs found on: • Multi-lane carriageways • Motorways
	7.3 Define different types of road furniture found on: • Multi-lane carriageways • Motorways
	7.4 Describe procedures for breakdowns on: • Multi-lane carriageways • Motorways
	7.5 Show own ability to estimate the speed of other vehicles.
	7.6 Anticipate other driver's actions and behaviours when driving.
	7.7 Drive safely on multi-lane carriageways and motorways.

Learning Outcome – The learner will:	Assessment Criteria – The learner can:
8. Be able to reverse and manoeuvre an ambulance vehicle safely.	8.1 Describe when a banksman is required when reversing.
	8.2 Use hand signals when acting as a banks man.
	8.3 Position a vehicle prior to a reversing manoeuvre.
	8.4 Reverse a vehicle to include: • All round observation • Appropriate use of vehicle controls • Judgement of vehicle position • Accuracy of manoeuvre • Spatial awareness • Demonstrate safe use of reversing aids

Learning Outcome – The learner will:	Assessment Criteria – The learner can:
9. Understand the use and effects of vehicle safety systems.	9.1 Describe different types and causes of skids.
	9.2 Describe how to avoid skids.
	9.3 Describe how the following vehicle safety systems work: • Electronic stability programme • ABS braking
	9.4 State procedures to maintain vehicle stability in a vehicle fitted with safety aids.
	9.5 State procedures to maintain vehicle stability in a vehicle not fitted with safety aids.

Learning Outcome – The learner will:	Assessment Criteria – The learner can:
10. Understand how to overtake other vehicles during routine driving.	10.1 Define legal requirements for passing vehicles during routine driving: • Overtaking • Passing on the left
	10.2 Explain the effects of vehicle performance and factors that will influence overtaking.
	10.3 Explain techniques for passing vehicles during routine driving: • Overtaking • Passing on the left

Learning Outcome – The learner will:	Assessment Criteria – The learner can:
11. Understand the effects of adverse conditions on driving.	11.1 Explain procedures for driving in the following conditions: • Fog • Ice • Rain • High winds • Snow

Learning Outcome – The learner will:	Assessment Criteria – The learner can:
12. Be able to manage confrontational behaviour whilst driving.	12.1 Identify situations where conflict involves: • Crew • Others • Other road users
	12.2 Identify human factors that are significant contributors to road traffic collisions.
	12.3 State the techniques to combat the effects of stress from confrontational behaviour whilst driving.
	12.4 Reflect on own driving practice during confrontational behaviour whilst driving

Learning Outcome – The learner will:	Assessment Criteria – The learner can:
13. Be able to navigate during routine driving.	13.1 Give directional information to colleague.
	13.2 Apply directional information from colleague.
	13.3 Use navigational aids safely to assist in routine driving.
	13.4 Manage distractions from within the vehicle whilst driving.

Unit 2: Drive Emergency Ambulance Vehicles

Unit Summary

This unit assesses the knowledge, skills and understanding required to drive an ambulance vehicle in emergency and non-emergency situations.

Learning Outcome – The learner will:	Assessment Criteria – The learner can:
1. Be able to use the system of car control.	1.1 Explain stages of the system of car control.
	1.2 Explain advantages of the system of car control.
	1.3 Describe how the system of car control works with different types of hazards.
	1.4 State the importance in a system of car control of: • Forward planning • Anticipation • Observation
	1.5 Describe the importance of a driving plan.
	1.6 Use the system of car control.

Learning Outcome – The learner will:	Assessment Criteria – The learner can:
2. Be able to use vehicles' transmission systems during emergency driving.	2.1 Explain the use of gears in relation to a progressive driving style.
	2.2 Select appropriate gears to drive in a progressive manner
	2.3 Use vehicle's transmission system effectively during progressive driving.

Learning Outcome – The learner will:	Assessment Criteria – The learner can:
3. Be able to overtake other vehicles during an emergency drive.	3.1 Explain the legal requirements for passing vehicles in an emergency: • Overtaking • Passing on the left
	3.2 Explain the effects of vehicle performance and factors to consider whilst overtaking.
	3.3 Explain techniques for passing vehicles in an emergency: • Overtaking • Passing on the left

| 3.4 Identify safe opportunities for overtaking in an emergency. |
| 3.5 Pass other vehicles in an emergency. |

Learning Outcome – The learner will:

4. Be able to drive an ambulance vehicle during hours of darkness in emergency and non-emergency situations.

Assessment Criteria – The learner can:
4.1 List requirements in vehicle preparation for driving in the hours of darkness.
4.2 Describe procedures for dealing with dazzle from other road users' lights.
4.3 Identify the symptoms of fatigue whilst driving during the hours of darkness.
4.4 Explain the procedures to take when affected by fatigue whilst driving during the hours of darkness.
4.5 Explain how driver's field of vision affects vehicle speed whilst driving during the hours of darkness.
4.6 Drive during the hours of darkness

Learning Outcome – The learner will:

5. Be able to drive in emergency response situations.

Assessment Criteria – The learner can:
5.1 List responsibilities of an emergency ambulance response driver.
5.2 Explain how audible and visual warnings can assist with safe progress.
5.3 Explain high speed driver training regulations.
5.4 Drive in compliance with high speed driver training regulations.
5.5 Manoeuvre the vehicle to facilitate a quick turnaround.
5.6 Explain situations when to use the following vehicle positions: • In line • Fend in • Fend off
5.7 State the techniques to combat the effects of stress when responding to emergencies.
5.8 Reflect on own driving practice in emergency response situations

Learning Outcome – The learner will:	**Assessment Criteria – The learner can:**
6. Be able to drive using exemptions for emergency ambulance response driving	6.1 Explain the exemptions available to ambulance vehicles whilst responding to emergency calls.
	6.2 Explain when to use exemptions in an emergency drive.
	6.3 Justify the use of exemptions when driving in an emergency.
	6.4 Drive using emergency ambulance response vehicle exemptions.

Learning Outcome – The learner will:	**Assessment Criteria – The learner can:**
7. Be able to manage confrontational behaviour when responding to emergencies.	7.1 Identify situations where conflict involves: • Crew • Others • Other road users
	7.2 Demonstrate ability to predict and safely respond to the behavioural changes of other drivers.

Learning Outcome – The learner will:	**Assessment Criteria – The learner can:**
8. Be able to navigate when responding to emergencies.	8.1 Give directional information to colleague.
	8.2 Apply directional information from colleague.
	8.3 Use navigational aids available to assist in an emergency response.
	8.4 Manage distractions from within the vehicle when responding to emergencies.

Appendix 4

Police Driver training

Becoming a police officer is a very popular career choice and is always over-subscribed. Each police service has its own recruitment process and selection policy. The first step is to contact the local police authority and request an application pack. As with any application for the emergency services, it is important to go over the detail very carefully before completing and returning the form.

Successful police candidates can expect intense interviews, physical examinations, written exercises and numerical and verbal tests. New recruits go through the same basic training programme, which is followed by a two year probation period, before becoming police constables.

Competition for selection is fierce. You can find help here:

*   www.how2become.com/courses/ultimate-day-1-police-assessment-training-course

Once your probation is complete you can make a choice of specialisation, quite possibly, to become a traffic police officer (TrafPol).

Police emergency drivers may be perceived to drive quickly, but they are trained to the highest standards with a matching discipline.

Traffic Police Driving courses

Police driver training regularly changes. Each police service provides various advanced driving courses to suit its own particular requirements. Civilian driving instructors may be used on courses, such as the standard emergency response course.

Standard Response Course

Students can expect to complete Category C1 (LGVs that weigh between 3½ and 7 tons) and D1 (Mini-buses up to 16 passenger seats) driving tests as precursors to the response course.

You can expect the response course to last around 2 weeks, including the Initial Phase Pursuit (IPP) element. Unmarked cars with covert blues may be used for this training.

Training for Police Support Units (PSU), that is the vans and carriers will be an additional week. Response graduates will be able to drive three classes of vehicle; car, van and PSU. They can also expect a probationary period before being signed off as competent. This is usually three months, because statistically, it is during this time when most police collisions (PolCol) happen.

The Advanced Course

This course is only available to existing police response drivers or those with special approval, such as members of the security forces or military personnel. It begins with theory and practical assessments using unmarked low powered cars. As the course progresses, students can expect a change of car; manual or automatic, each with high engine power.

Cost savings have meant that the time spend on these courses has been reduced. At the Metropolitan Police Driving School at Hendon, it is now only three weeks long.

Course assessments will vary according to the service, but is likely to include simulated blue light runs. The "Class 1" and "Class 2" police classification grades are no longer used by all services. Instead, the assessments are competency based, the outcome being "Police Advanced Driver". Limits may be put on officers as to what vehicles they can drive operationally in what circumstances.

Having graduated to "Advanced" classification, drivers must take refresher check-tests every 3-5 years.

Tactical Pursuit & Containment (TPAC) Course

The National Police Chiefs' Council (NPCC) has now replaced the Association of Chief Police Officers (ACPO). The NPCC requires all police services to provide TPAC training.

TPAC deals with the drivers of vehicles that fail to stop voluntarily, "ram raiders" and the resolution of firearms incidents. Any pursuit is managed working to a plan, maintaining an element of control. Devices such as "Stinger" may be incorporated into the tactics. This course runs for a week and can only be attended by Advanced traffic officers. Once TPAC trained, the first refresher must take place within 24 months, then every 12 months.

Other driving courses

Police driving schools also provide motorcycle training, Large Goods Vehicle (LGV) and Passenger Carrying Vehicle (PCV) Courses as well as off road courses for motorcycle and car.

The Metropolitan Police are the only service to provide an Anti-Hijack Protection Driving Course. This provides the necessary skills, including high-speed reversing, to help officers escape from ambush style situations.

Each driving course described here is designed to equip officers with the knowledge and skills required for effective operational deployment and meet the needs of policing in Britain.

Appendix 5

Driver training with the Fire and Rescue Service

Having decided that fire-fighting is the career for you, the process of joining the service varies throughout the UK but the joining principles remain pretty much the same.   Find out when your local Fire and Rescue Service are recruiting for firefighters. A web search for this information, along with a visit to your local Fire Station should be your first actions.

All the details you need, including advice on completing the application form, to figuring out the best way to get ahead of other candidates, can be found at:

*   www.fireservice.co.uk/recruitment/howtojoin

Competition for selection is fierce. You can find help on this website:

*   www.how2become.com/courses/firefighter

Within the Fire Service, Emergency Response Driver (ERD) training varies according to geographic location and available resource. The courses are based on nationally agreed competencies.

The fire appliance is a rigid Large Goods Vehicle (LGV), Category C. Unless you have this entitlement already on your driving license, you will first need to add provisional entitlement to your current driving license. To do this, you will need an application form from the Driver Vehicle Licensing Agency (DVLA). For this to be accepted, you must take and pass a medical examination. This can be performed by your own doctor. Fees are involved for this process.

The Emergency Fire Appliance Driver (EFAD) training course

Not all members of the fire crew on a tender are necessarily trained to drive the appliance or other vehicles on emergency response.

Before driver-training can start, the fire-fighter must have successfully completed a probationary period. Once nominated for EFAD training by Watch Officers or Station Commanders, potential students should expect to pass a technical exam before starting their training.

The length and format of an EFAD course will vary according to the particular fire service. A "typical" initial driver training course can take 7 days.

The first 2 days are spent in a car, to learn the basics of "Roadcraft"; including the "System of Vehicle Control". During this time, the skid-training element can be presented as a theory session. The view being that students need to be trained in how to avoid the skid from happening in the first place, rather than teaching them how to get out of it. Some fire services do however provide practical skid-training for their students.

The next 5 days are spent on a fire appliance. There are normally two students per instructor, though the ratio may be one to one. Most fire services have delegated DVSA driving examiners who conduct an official driving test on the final day. Driving instructors, as you would expect, monitor each student's progress through continuous assessment. If a student is not yet ready for test, then it can be postponed. This accounts for the better-than-industry pass rate.

Once the student has passed their LGV test, the training programme continues at the fire station for a period of about 6 months. During this time, each student needs to typically complete at least 300 miles worth of driving experience in varying road, traffic, weather, daylight and night-time conditions in a "fully laden" appliance.

Between the LGV and Emergency Response Course (ERC), students are expected to complete a theory programme based on "Roadcraft". Knowledge checks are performed as part of the course. Students are also expected to complete a daily log. This reflects feelings on how they are progressing, along with areas where more work needs to be done. This is then endorsed by the instructor, overseen by the station commander.

The ERC course will be in the appliance, over the period of one or two weeks. In anticipation of the implementation of Section 19 of the Road Safety Act (2006), the assessment criteria are based on that standard. This can be found in Appendix 1 of this Guide.

Depending on the Fire Service's choice, EFAD training course accreditations can be provided by RoSPA or the IAM. This is for external quality assurance purposes.

Since 2012, the London Fire Brigade (LFB) have outsourced their training to the engineering support service company, Babcocks International Group PLC. This company also provides training for other fire and rescue services, including Devon & Somerset, Avon, Gloucester and South Wales. The majority of fire services still deliver "in-house" training.

Becoming a firefighter can take many months, or even years applying and getting prepared prior for gaining entry. Potential students should be patient with the process. A career within the Fire and Rescue Service holds many rewards and in some rural areas, there are joint roles with the ambulance service.

Finally, students must be prepared to work very hard, in every aspect, as well as their driving skills. As you might imagine, these will be checked, usually every three to five years.

Appendix 6

Scene Management at Road Traffic Collisions (RTC)

Ambulance Service Vehicle – In Line / Fend off / Fend In

When arriving at an emergency call to an incident on a motorway or multi-lane carriageway, crew safety is paramount. If a traffic situation is unsafe, the crew cannot render aid.

Ambulance vehicles will usually position beyond the incident. Where the police are not yet in attendance, before leaving the vehicle, the ambulance driver has to make a dynamic risk assessment. This will include:

1. Location

    • Position/visibility – is the incident position dangerous, eg, in lane 3 or on a bend?

    • Characteristics – is the location on an elevated slip or in roadworks?

2. Vehicles

    • Number and type involved?

    • Condition – damage and extent and is any part of the vehicle or load obviously dangerous?

Radio a "Situation Report" through to Control, including the above information and number of the nearest distance marker post. On a motorway these are installed at 100 metre intervals alongside the hard shoulder.

Until the arrival of the police, liveried ambulance vehicles can be used to offer scene protection. **Advice on this will be subject to Service Policy.**

Assuming that the front-end of the ambulance is pointing in the direction of normal travel, the main methods of positioning a vehicle are:

• **In Line.** This is a position parallel to the running lanes on the carriageway. This maximises rear-facing lighting and rear vehicle markings. When parking straight on a hard shoulder, without a crash barrier, turn the steering wheels to face inwards.

- **Fend-off.** The vehicle is angled, pointing front end towards the offside, in the direction that the traffic should pass. The vehicle position should cover the affected lane and one lane either side of this, for example, where the incident is in lane 2, cover lanes 1 & 2.

- **Fend-in.** The vehicle is angled, pointing front end toward the nearside, in the direction the traffic should pass. The vehicle position should cover the affected lane and one lane either side of this, for example, where the incident is in lane 3, cover lanes 2 & 3.

Emergency vehicles should be positioned at a minimum of 50 metres to the rear of the incident. The steering wheels should be turned so that a rear-end collision would avoid the vehicle being pushed into a precarious position that could jeopardise the safety of any persons. On multi-lane carriageways, on no account should the incident scene and responders form an island with traffic passing on both sides.

Once safely positioned, where fitted, activate the RUN LOCK and ARRIVAL MODE functions. For vehicles without the ARRIVAL MODE, activate "REAR REDS" manually (if fitted). Turn off headlight flashers.

Outside the vehicle, all crew members must wear Personal Protective Equipment (fasten up hi-visibility long sleeve jacket and wear helmet). When collecting equipment, use the side door of the ambulance and try to avoid turning your back on passing traffic. Once the police arrive, they will manage the scene and ambulance vehicles can be moved to the safe side of the incident.

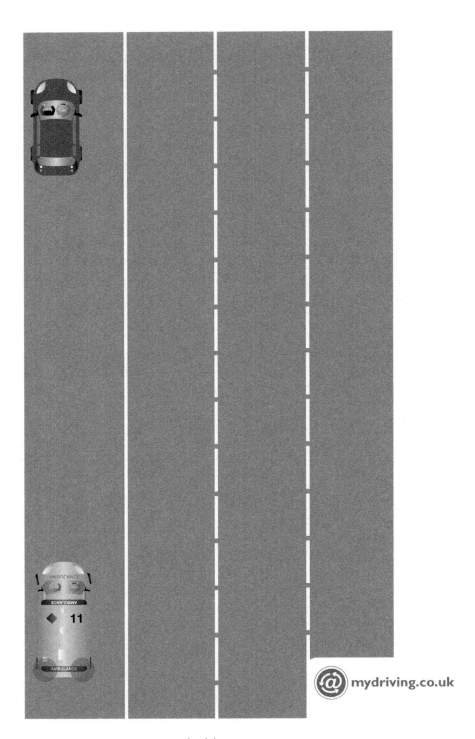

In Line

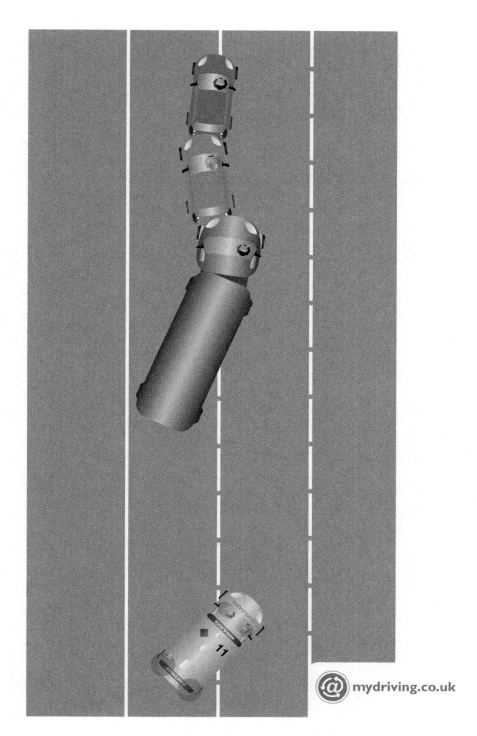

Fend Off

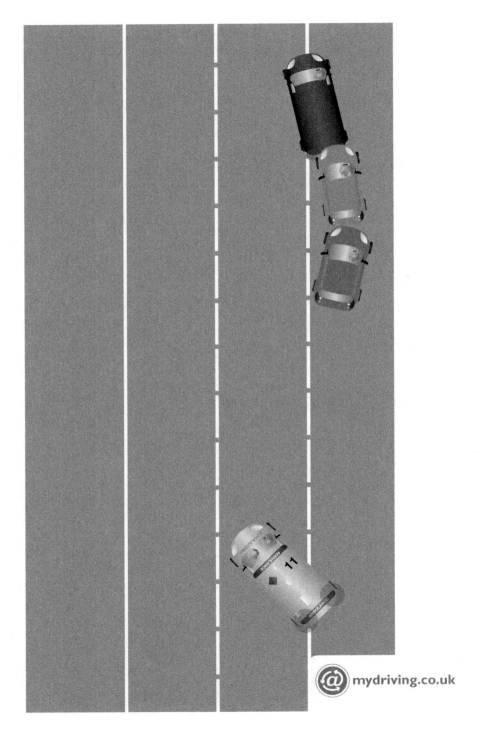

Fend In

Appendix 7

Glossary of Commonest Abbreviations and Terms

AACE	Association of Ambulance Chief Executives
ABS	Anti-Lock Braking System
A&E	Accident and Emergency Department of the Hospital
AIRSO	Association of Industrial Road Safety Officers
ANPR	Automatic Number Plate Recognition
ARV	Armed Response Vehicle
ATS	Automatic Traffic Signals
AVLS	Automatic Vehicle Locating System
Blue Call	Emergency response using blue lights and sirens
BTP	British Transport Police
Control	Call centre that dispatches the response drivers
COLP	City of London Police
CSR	Core Skills Review
DfT	Department for Transport
DMA	Double Manned Ambulance
DTAG	Driver Training and Advisory Group (Ambulance Service)
DVLA	Driver & Vehicle Licensing Agency
DVSA	Driver Vehicle Standards Agency
DRA	Dynamic Risk Assessment
ECA	Emergency Care Assistant
ECSW	Emergency Care and Support Worker
ESC	Electronic Stability Control
ESP	Electronic Stability Programme
EMT	Emergency Medical Technician
EFAD	Emergency Fire Appliance Driver
Frequent Flyer	A regular caller of the emergency services
FPN	Fixed Penalty Notice
FRU	Fast Response Unit
HART	Hazardous Area Response Team
HEMS	Helicopter Emergency Medical Services
HSDT	High Speed Driver Training
IAM	Institute of Advanced Motorists

IC	Identification Code
IDR	Incident Data Recorder
IHCD	Institute of Health Care Development (Edexcel)
IRV	Incident Response Vehicle
LED	Light emitting Diode
LESLP	London Emergency Services Liaison Panel
LFB	London Fire Brigade
Loc Match	Location Match. The address for the call has a history
MDT	Mobile Data Terminal
MDP	Ministry of Defence Police
NIP	Notice of Impending Prosecution
NPCC	National Police Chief's Council
NSL	National Speed Limit
One Under	Someone has either fallen or jumped under a moving train
PDC	Pre-Driving Checks
PNC	Police National Computer
PPE	Personal Protective Equipment
QA	Quality Assurance
RoSPA	Royal Society for the Prevention of Accidents
RTA/C	Road Traffic Accident/Collision
Running Call	Where a response crew come across an incident, without being called
RVP	Rendezvous Point
SRV	Single Response Vehicle
PolCol	Police Collision
PDC	Pre-Driving Check
Shout	Police term for an emergency response using blue lights and sirens
TC	Traction Control
TEAC	Trainee Emergency Ambulance Crew
TrafPol	Traffic Police
VDI	Vehicle Daily Inspection

Appendix 8

Useful Contacts

This is a list of the organisations that are mostly likely to be able to assist you to develop your own driving standards.

High Performance Course (HPC)

The High Performance Course will set you on the road to become one of the safest and best civilian road drivers in the country. HPC coaches have been Police trained to the highest level. Course graduates share a common value set. They are passionate about driving, open minded and committed to learning and self-improvement. Preparation for HPC is essential, in the form of taking training for the IAM and or RoSPA Tests first.

Course graduates are invited to join the exclusive High Performance Club. For more details, contact HPC through their website:

www.high-performance-course.com

Contact details on website

Magazine: High Performance Club News

Institute of Advanced Motorists (IAM)

The IAM is a road safety charity based in Chiswick, West London. The organisation has more than two hundred voluntary affiliated groups around the country. Individual members of these groups have taken and passed the advanced test and often make themselves available to help others do the same.

Institute of Advanced Motorists
510 Chiswick High Road
London, W4 5RG
T: 020 8996 9600
E: info@iam.org.uk
W: www.iam.org.uk
Magazine: Advanced Driving

Royal Society for the Prevention of Accidents (RoSPA)

RoSPA's Advanced Drivers' and Riders' Association is a charity based in Birmingham. They have a network of over 50 local groups around the UK. These groups have trained and experienced tutors willing to offer free advice, assessments and support to help drivers and motorcyclists prepare for their Advanced Driving/Motorcycling test.

Royal Society for the Prevention of Accidents
28 Calthorpe House
Edgbaston
Birmingham, B15 1RP
T: 0121 248 2000
E: help@rospa.com
W: www.rospa.com
Magazine: Care on the Road

Association of Industrial Road Safety Officers (AIRSO)

AIRSO is also a charity.　It is an independent membership organisation working in the interests of road safety, highly respected in the field within the public, private and voluntary sectors. Members represent a wide cross-section, including commercial transport, fleet management, driver training, independent and local government road safety organisations, the armed services, the emergency services and enforcement agencies. Membership of AIRSO is open to any person whose work is in any way connected with the promotion of road safety.

Association of Industrial Road safety Officers (AIRSO)
Brook Haven, Three Cocks
Brecon, LD3 0SN
T: 01497 842708
E: sandra@airso.org.uk
W: www.airso.org.uk
EZINE: AIRSO Communication (Frequent bulletins)

INDEX